WHEATON PUBLIC LI[BRARY]
882.09 LEN
Lenson, David,
The birth of tragedy :a con

P9-DCP-603

3 5143 00147650 6

WN

882.09 LEN

Lenson, David

The birth of tragedy

AUG   1988

MAY   1991

DEC   1992

Wheaton Public Library
225 N. Cross
Wheaton, Illinois   60187

THE BIRTH OF TRAGEDY

—— A Commentary ——

TWAYNE'S MASTERWORK STUDIES
Robert Lecker, General Editor

THE BIRTH OF TRAGEDY

—— A Commentary ——

DAVID LENSON

TWAYNE PUBLISHERS • BOSTON
A Division of G.K. Hall & Co.

The Birth of Tragedy: A Commentary
David Lenson

Twayne's Masterwork Studies
No. 8

Copyright 1987 by G.K. Hall & Co.
All rights reserved.
Published by Twayne Publishers
A Division of G.K. Hall & Co.
70 Lincoln Street
Boston, Massachusetts 02111

Copyediting supervised by Lewis DeSimone

Typeset in 10/14 Sabon with Bodoni display type.
by Compset, Inc.

Printed on permanent/durable acid-free paper
and bound in the United States of America

Excerpt from Thomas Mann, *Death in Venice
and Seven Other Stories*, trans. H. T. Lowe-Porter
(New York: Knopf, 1936), 67–68, reprinted by
permission of Alfred A. Knopf, Inc. Copyright
1936 by Alfred A. Knopf, Inc.

Library of Congress Cataloging in Publication Data

Lenson, David, 1945–
    The birth of tragedy.

    (Twayne's masterwork studies ; no. 8)
    Bibliography: p.
    Includes index.
    1. Nietzsche, Friedrich Wilhelm, 1844–1900.
Geburt der Tragödie. 2. Aesthetics. 3. Music—
Philosophy and aesthetics. 4. Tragedy. 5. Greek
drama (Tragedy)—History and criticism. 6. Tragic, The.
7. Wagner, Richard, 1813–1883. I. Title. II. Series.
B3313.G43L46   1987   111'.85   87-12101
ISBN 0-8057-7968-X
    0-8057-8008-4 (pbk.)

CONTENTS

NOTE ON REFERENCES

I have used the translation of Walter Kaufmann, published in 1967 by Random House and still easily available, throughout this commentary. Its clarity and scholarly apparatus make it generally superior to the rather more lyrical and passionate rendition by Francis Golffing, published by Doubleday in 1956.

Kaufmann's translation was based upon Elisabeth Förster-Nietzsche's second Leipzig edition, published between 1905 and 1910, and the Munich Musarion edition of 1920–29. Since Kaufmann's version, a new *Werke, Kritische Gesamtausgabe* has been in progress, edited by G. Colli and M. Montinari (Berlin and New York: De Gruyter, 1967–). For daily reference, I have used a paperback edition published by Wilhelm Goldmann Verlag in Munich. This text is, however, based upon the earlier Förster-Nietzsche edition and is therefore not reliable for research.

CHRONOLOGY: FRIEDRICH NIETZSCHE'S LIFE AND WORKS

1844	Friedrich Nietzsche is born on 15 October in Röcken, Prussian Saxony, the son of Karl Ludwig Nietzsche (b. 1813), a Lutheran pastor, and Franziska Oehler Nietzsche (b. 1826).
1846	His sister, Elisabeth, is born on 10 July.
1848	His brother, Joseph, is born in February.
1849	Karl Ludwig Nietzsche dies on 30 July, leaving Friedrich with only the dimmest memory of his father.
1850	Joseph Nietzsche dies in January, and the family moves to Naumburg, a somewhat larger town. Nietzsche's formal education begins in a local elementary school.
1855	Nietzsche transfers to another school, the Dom Gymnasium near Naumburg.
1858	He is accepted as a student at the prestigious Pforta boarding school and matriculates in October. This proves to be a crucial event in Nietzsche's life, as the traditional but superior quality of Pforta gives him a strong foundation, particularly in classical languages, for his subsequent academic life.
1859	Nietzsche begins to write, working on a play about Prometheus.
1860	He begins composing music.
1861	Nietzsche suffers a serious illness in February, the first in a life of bad health, and is sent home from school. In March he undergoes confirmation. During this year he writes his first essays.
1862	Despite another illness in the summer, Nietzsche produces two essays and a dramatic fragment.
1864	In the fall, Nietzsche matriculates at Bonn University to study classical philology and theology. He writes an essay on the

classical Greek poet Theognis and reads David Strauss's *Life of Jesus*, a book that affects his thinking about Christianity for some time. He also fights a duel, an obligatory ritual in the life of a young Prussian male, and gains a scar to show for it.

1865   In a dramatic gesture, Nietzsche refuses to take communion at Easter, causing great consternation in his family. He discovers the philosophy of Arthur Schopenhauer, one of his most lasting influences. In the fall, he transfers to Leipzig University, following his favorite teacher, Albrecht Ritschl.

1867   Nietzsche begins his long friendship with Erwin Rohde. He continues writing and researching the Greek philosophers Diogenes and Democritus until he is conscripted for military service in October. A famous incident occurs at this time: Falling off a horse during a training exercise, hanging on to the saddle underneath his mount, Nietzsche reportedly cries out in fear, "Schopenhauer! Help me now!"

1868   Nietzsche has a riding accident in March and is discharged from the army in October with a serious chest wound that disables him once again. Learning to work despite physical pain, he writes an essay on teleology. Finally recovered, he has his first meeting with Richard Wagner in Leipzig in November. During the next few years, Wagner and his wife, Cosima, become his artistic and intellectual mentors, and a kind of surrogate family.

1869   In January Nietzsche receives his astonishing appointment to Basel University in Switzerland. In April he takes Swiss citizenship, which he retains for the rest of his life. On 17 May he pays his first visit to the Wagners at their mansion, Tribschen. He gives his introductory lecture at Basel, entitled "Homer and Classical Philology," on 28 May.

1870   Despite his youth, he becomes a full professor in March. He gives two impressive lectures, one on Greek music-drama and another on Socrates and tragedy. Both of these are important early explorations of the themes of *The Birth of Tragedy*. He serves briefly as a medical orderly in the Franco-Prussian War, but in the harsh conditions of combat falls ill again and returns to Basel in October, around the time of the French surrender.

1871   Already feeling constrained by the discipline of philology, Nietzsche tries to transfer to a chair in philosophy, but encounters difficulties of academic politics. In April he completes *The Birth of Tragedy*. In November the manuscript is accepted for publication by Ernst Wilhelm Fritzsche, Wagner's pub-

	lisher. Wagner is somewhat annoyed, thinking the book would have greater credibility were it taken by a more conventional academic house.
1872	*The Birth of Tragedy* is published, and the famous battle of the reviewers ensues. In April the Wagners return to Germany from their long exile and prepare to lay the cornerstone of the great theater at Bayreuth. In June a musical composition by Nietzsche gets a rebuff from Wagner's conductor (and Cosima's first husband) Hans von Bulow, and Nietzsche effectively gives up composing music as a serious pursuit.
1873	Nietzsche's chronic eye trouble begins. The first two *Untimely Meditations* are published.
1874	Nietzsche continues working on the third *Untimely Meditation*. This year marks the beginning of his split with Wagner, as the Master takes offense when Nietzsche leaves a score by Brahms on his piano.
1875	He publishes the fourth *Untimely Meditation*, entitled "Richard Wagner in Bayreuth."
1876	Increasingly unhealthy, Nietzsche takes a leave of absence from his professorship in February. In the summer, he makes his disillusioning journey to the opening festivities at Bayreuth. In November he has his last meeting with Wagner.
1878	In January Nietzsche sends the first part of *Human, All-Too-Human* to the publisher, completing the second part at the end of the year. This work contains Nietzsche's first public repudiation of Wagner, and in September the composer counterattacks. In this year, Nietzsche's most productive period begins, as do his incessant wanderings throughout Europe in search of a climate that will alleviate his physical sufferings. From this point on, Nietzsche is never really healthy again.
1879	Nietzsche formally resigns from Leipzig University in May. Part 3 of *Human, All-Too-Human* is published in December.
1880	Nietzsche works on *Sunrise*.
1881	*Sunrise* is completed in February. Nietzsche begins *Thus Spoke Zarathustra* and *The Gay Science*.
1882	*The Gay Science* is published in August. From April through November, his famous friendship with Lou Salome takes place. This is the single amorous episode in his otherwise ascetic life, and it causes him lasting pain.
1883	Wagner dies, and Nietzsche is unabashedly relieved. The first book of *Zarathustra* is completed in January.

1884	He finishes book 2 of *Zarathustra*.
1885	On 22 May his sister, Elisabeth, marries Bernhard Förster, an anti-Semitic crusader who plans to found an Aryan utopia in Paraguay. Nietzsche is very disturbed by this union.
1886	He completes *Beyond Good and Evil* in January, and it is published in August. Elisabeth and Förster leave for Paraguay. Nietzsche sees his friend Erwin Rohde for the last time.
1887	Nietzsche writes and publishes *The Genealogy of Morals*.
1888	During his last miraculous year of conscious life, Nietzsche writes *The Antichrist, Dionysus Dithyrambs, The Case Of Wagner, Twilight Of The Idols, Ecce Homo*, and several lesser works.
1889	Just after the first of the year, Nietzsche attempts to intercede when he sees a horse being beaten in the streets of Turin, Italy. He undergoes a seizure and collapse from which he never recovers. Brought back to Basel by his friend Franz Overbeck, he enters a clinic where hope for his recovery is soon abandoned. In June his brother-in-law, Förster, commits suicide in Paraguay when he is shown to be embezzling money from his community.
1890	In March Nietzsche, reduced to a husk of a man, is released from the clinic and lives with his mother in Jena. Elisabeth returns from Paraguay in December and resolves to devote the rest of her life to promoting her brother's work.
1892	Elisabeth prepares an inexpensive popular edition of Nietzsche's works and then returns to Paraguay to conclude her business there. Nietzsche begins to receive considerable recognition, but is completely unaware of it.
1893	Elisabeth returns from Paraguay and founds the Nietzsche Archive. From this point on, she is in full charge of all Nietzsche's manuscripts and notebooks, a curatorship that many scholars feel did both Nietzsche's reputation and his literary estate serious damage.
1896	Elisabeth moves the Archive to Weimar.
1900	Nietzsche dies on 25 August.

1

HISTORICAL CONTEXT

Friedrich Nietzsche, as he was writing *The Birth of Tragedy*, was still working within the confines of the German academy, a world of which he was an exemplary product. He had the distinction of being one of the most noteworthy *students* of his age. His maturation as a philosopher may be correlated with his departure from academic life, which was finalized with his formal resignation from Basel in 1879. The highly controversial nature of *The Birth of Tragedy* indicates that Nietzsche was already in rebellion against the discipline of philology even at the outset of his professorship. At the time he was putting the finishing touches on the book, he was engaging in a difficult piece of academic politicking, trying to change his appointment from philology to philosophy, a maneuver almost impossible in the rigid compartmentalization of his university.

For these reasons, the real background of this book is to be found in the histories of philosophy and philology, as much as in the history of political events. To take account of this philosophical background is a lengthy project, which I have attempted in the first two sections of the main commentary. There is no question, however, that the German victory in the Franco-Prussian War, coming just as

Nietzsche was composing his book, had a profound impact upon *The Birth of Tragedy*. It actually interrupted Nietzsche's writing of preliminary versions of the book; for although he had done his obligatory military service in peacetime in 1867 and 1868, he was roused sufficiently by the declaration of war to volunteer as a medical orderly in August 1870—an effort that ended in October as his health once again failed, just before the French army surrendered. In his preface to the 1886 edition of *The Birth of Tragedy*, Nietzsche explicitly associates his book with "the exciting time of the Franco-Prussian War of 1860/71."

Nietzsche was, after all, a Prussian for the first twenty-four and a half years of his life, and much of the nationalist rhetoric in the second half of *The Birth of Tragedy* may be ascribed to Prussia's triumph in the war with France, with all its implications for the future of Europe. Previously a disunified group of Protestant states lying north of the Catholic Austro-Hungarian Empire, Germany in the modern sense did not exist until 18 January 1871, when Bismarck proclaimed the formation of the German Empire in the Hall of Mirrors at Versailles, deep inside occupied France. This new state, springing full-blown from the Prussian victory, immediately became the most powerful force in a changing Europe. Controlling the northern continent all the way from Alsace-Lorraine to the Russian frontier, the proclamation of the Empire was more than a consolidation of economic, military, and political power. It was also an unparalleled cultural event. It satisfied a longstanding popular desire for a Protestant German nation that would overcome internal division, achieve an integral civilization, and gain the respect of the rest of Europe and the world.

Nietzsche could only dimly foresee the results of German unification, since he finished his manuscript only three months after Versailles. It is perhaps difficult for a present-day reader, knowing the dreadful history of Germany through two world wars, to understand the excitement that greeted the new Empire. Certainly, Nietzsche's enthusiasm was short-lived. Even before the completion of his manuscript, he was already expressing uneasiness in his private correspondence. Soon enough, he would use his Swiss citizenship, which he retained for the rest of his life, as leverage to dissociate himself from Germany, which immediately following the proclamation underwent a period of industrial development that still stands out as one of the most vigorous in modern history, on a par, perhaps, with that of Japan following World War II. The overwhelming materialism of those times, along with the sudden growth of the previously dormant German bourgeoisie, became for Nietzsche an uncommonly clear manifestation of "herd mentality," and he spared no effort in attacking it throughout the maturity of his career.

Given his youth and the straitness of his Prussian, Protestant upbringing, Nietzsche can hardly be blamed for succumbing to the euphoria of Versailles. There was also a personal symbol for him in the fact that Richard Wagner was shortly to be allowed to return from his long exile, which had begun after his involvement in the Dresden uprising of 1848. All of the latter half of *The Birth of Tragedy*, with its assertions about Wagner's potential for reviving Aeschylean tragedy in Germany, may seem narrow and jingoistic at times, but it is part and parcel of the feeling among German people that a great common adventure of limitless potential was about to begin.

Even as preparations for the proclamation were taking place at Versailles, the Prussians were holding the city of Paris under siege. After France's loss and the capture of Napoleon III, a new Republic had been proclaimed in Paris along radically democratic, even socialist lines. Known as the Paris Commune, it was later recognized by Lenin as the first revolutionary socialist state in the history of the world, a predecessor of his own Bolshevik Russia. Although the Commune lasted only four months, until starving and exhausted Parisians yielded the city to the German army, even in defeat it became a powerful symbol of the hopes of socialists and radical democrats; indeed, it remains so today. Even in Bismarck's new Germany, Marx and Lassalle would shortly form the Social Democratic Party (1875), after which the "spectre of Communism" that Marx and Engels said was haunting Europe as early as 1848 would never go away. Bismarck, in order to combat the half-million votes polled by Marx's party in a parliamentary election of 1877, was forced to concede certain democratic reforms even as he enacted a series of "Exceptional Laws" (1878–90) to constrict the socialists.

It is therefore reasonable to say that modern socialism was born in the same spasm that produced modern Germany. To put it dramatically, "The International" was written in the same year as *The Birth of Tragedy*. Nietzsche regarded socialism (and democracy—the terms were not yet entirely separate) as still another manifestation of that "herd mentality" he so dreaded. He saw egalitarianism as a great leveler, threatening to do away with excellence of all sorts. Since socialism was inextricably bound up with Christian thought in the early nineteenth century, particularly in France, Nietzsche was to regard it as embodying many of the objectionable qualities of that "slave religion," bringing its imperatives (such as the Golden Rule, for example, or Jesus' overturning of the moneylenders' tables) into the political arena. Undoubtedly, Nietzsche felt for a short while after Versailles that the new German Empire would serve as an effective bulwark against socialism, as indeed it did for a time.

It is possible to connect Nietzsche's disillusionment with Germany to the crisis point in his schism with Wagner, that is, to the inauguration of Wagner's *Festspielhaus* in Bayreuth in 1876. Here was the moment Nietzsche had predicted four and a half years earlier would be the modern counterpart of the opening of the City Dionysia in ancient Athens. Yet all the philosopher felt was profound disappointment. The audience attracted by this great event was drawn from the rising industrial upper-middle class. It was neither aristocratic (which Nietzsche would have accepted) nor popular in a way that would offer a broad-based alternative to democracy and socialism. Its seats were filled with as affluent, crass, and insensitive an audience as would have filled any other contemporary opera house. They were there to be seen, because this was the new "official culture" of the Empire. Thereafter, Nietzsche would be hard-pressed to say a good word about either Wagner or Germany.

It would be possible to make an interpretation of Nietzsche's work based upon his alienation from the particular form that political modernization and the industrial revolution took in Germany. *The Birth of Tragedy*, from this perspective, is merely a point of departure; it could be read as a document reflecting the fondest hopes of nationalism—which at the time was still perceived as a progressive ideology—for cultural renewal. Although this historical approach will not be emphasized in the commentary that follows, it is in fact inescapable for understanding what may otherwise appear to be the rather narrower second half of the book.

2

THE IMPORTANCE OF THE WORK

There are several reasons to read *The Birth of Tragedy*. First of all, it is the earliest major work of Friedrich Nietzsche. Second, it has exercised a stronger influence on theory and criticism of Greek tragedy than any work since Aristotle's *Poetics,* with G. W. F. Hegel's *Lectures on Aesthetics* as its only modern rival. Third, it is of interest to musicologists because of its relationship to the work of Richard Wagner. But finally, it is a discursive work that transcends its own genre and subject, and resonates beyond itself into ethics and theology. This is what gives it an unassailable place in the history of thought.

As an introduction to the philosophy of Nietzsche, *The Birth of Tragedy* is both illuminating and misleading. This is because it contains preliminary versions of ideas that eventually became his major preoccupations. Both Dionysus and Socrates, for example, recur throughout his later work with ever-changing resonances. Though it may sound silly to say so, this book functions as an introduction to Nietzsche's philosophy only if the reader actually goes on to the rest. It is very different from Nietzsche's aphoristic middle works, his prophetic *Thus Spoke Zarathustra,* or his painfully personal final volumes. Partly this is a matter of style. In 1872 Nietzsche was still writing within an academic context, although he had already grown far too broad-voiced for his colleagues in philology. He continued to grow as a writer throughout his brief career, always expanding his stylistic range, and there is much about *The Birth of Tragedy* that is still unformed. It is also true that Nietzsche is not yet fully mature as a *thinker* in this early work. The marks left by his mentors—especially Schopenhauer and Wagner—are still too fresh, as he himself would acknowledge in late reappraisals of the book. *The Birth of Tragedy* is therefore necessary, but hardly sufficient, for an understanding of the whole Nietzsche.

In the field of theory of tragedy, it stands on its own. It challenges the plot-oriented approach that had dominated the field since Hegel. Nietzsche's idea of a religious and musical origin of Greek drama offers some explanation for the enduring emotional power of tragic conflict and for the presence of the chorus, which many theorists had reduced to a merely ancillary role. Taken in tandem with Sir James Frazer's *The Golden Bough*, *The Birth of Tragedy* spawned the misnamed Cambridge Anthropological School (misnamed because one of its principals, Gilbert Murray, was in fact an Oxonian), which set out to investigate Nietzsche's propositions in a more rigorous way. It influenced even Marxists like George Thomson, and it has recently been subjected to compendious reassessment as part of a general revival of interest in Nietzsche. This book has become similar to one of its own targets, Aristotle's *Poetics*, in that all subsequent theory of tragedy must take it into account.

While discussing the origin of tragedy in Greek antiquity, Nietzsche was also preparing a brief for Richard Wagner. The young Nietzsche thought of himself as a composer; it took specific discouragement to prevent him from continuing. *The Birth of Tragedy* is partly an attempt to promote Wagner's music and amplify his ideas about art, especially those in *Opera and Drama* (1851). It was this aspect of the book that received the most initial attention. Indeed, it took Nietzsche quite some time, and a complete personal and intellectual break with Wagner, to escape the stigmatic designation of "literary Wagnerianism."

As for the book's status as a landmark in the history of thought, I recollect my own initial undergraduate reading. I found in it not only a view of tragedy spectacularly different from the one I had been taught, but also a radical analysis of consciousness itself, devolving upon the opposition of Apollo and Dionysus, and their collective opposition to Socrates. The ethical queries that would someday take Nietzsche "beyond good and evil" are already here—that is, two contrary views of life are presented without the denigration of either. The revelation that ethics need not be merely judgmental struck me at once. Dionysus and Apollo became figures for *modes of being*, as it were. As I exhausted a yellow felt underliner on my rapidly replaced first copy, I was moved by Nietzsche's passionate belief in art as indispensable for life itself.

Any sensitive first reader will see at once that this is more than a work of literary criticism, more than a defense of Wagner, more than the juvenilia of a great philosopher. It is a book that asks profound questions about civilization, taking as its starting point one of our earliest cultural institutions—tragedy. Why tragedy? Partly, of course, because it was one of the subjects regularly treated by philologists, but more significantly because tragedy is inescapably about conflict—as is civilization itself. The occasional concurrence of Nietzsche's thought with Freud's hinges upon this insight.

Perhaps the immediacy and power of *The Birth of Tragedy*, as in Nietzsche's later works, stem from one innovation above all: the embodiment of ideas, even large complexes of connected ideas, into gods or historical figures. Apollo, Dionysus, Socrates, Zarathustra, Wagner, Schopenhauer, and the Overman are all characters in a drama of ideas, an art form of the intellect that is neither mere allegory nor systematic philosophy. The only antecedent, acknowledged by Nietzsche himself, is Ralph Waldo Emerson, whose essays aspired not to logical cohesion but to "spires of form." Emerson's "Representative Men" and figures such as the Poet and the American Scholar, are, like Nietzsche's characters, not merely mythic or historical portmanteaux, but ideas-come-to-life. Through the creation of such figures, Nietzsche illustrates his belief in the emotional foundation of all ideas. There is nothing detached or disinterested about *The Birth of Tragedy;* it is a work animated by passion and visionary intuition. Its importance lies in the fact that, from the day of its publication, the universe of Western thought has never been the same.

3

CRITICAL RECEPTION

Nietzsche received his doctorate from Leipzig University in the field of philology. Since philology no longer exists per se in modern universities, a brief look at this discipline may be helpful in understanding why the publication of *The Birth of Tragedy* caused such a memorable scholarly controversy.

Philology comes from the Greek, meaning "love of words." It came into being as part of eighteenth century Germany's sudden fascination with Greek antiquity, exemplified by the work of Johann Joachim Winckelmann (1717–68). German scholars in effect decided that they would undertake the preservation of Greek literature, just as Italian scholars had done for Latin. Accordingly, they began the daunting task of locating and cataloging Greek codices in order to prepare definitive editions. They compared the various manuscripts of a given literary work and provided an *apparatus criticus* noting the manuscripts' discrepancies. They reconstructed flawed passages and indicated which possible readings were the soundest. The impressive compendia they produced read like encoded messages, employing a mysterious and elaborate shorthand reminiscent of the one scrawled by physicians on prescription forms. Philologists also furnished commentaries on their texts. Most of the time these treated unusual usages of words or idioms, aiming to elucidate peculiar phrases by finding analogous instances in other texts. For example, a bit of Aeschylean syntax might be explicated by means of a comparison with a passage from Pindar.

Philology, as its name indicates, was a method for studying language. It differed from contemporary linguistics in that its objects of study were exclusively literary. Philologists needed a vast knowledge of one or more languages and their literatures, and therefore the field required extensive graduate training. Furthermore, it was rigorously "scientific" in its treatment of literature, regarding texts principally as illustrations of linguistic phenomena, and scarcely at all as imaginative works. It was one of the more successful attempts to impose the rigors and standards of natural science upon the wilderness of creative language, and therefore it adhered to its method quite stubbornly.

When Nietzsche, at so extraordinarily early an age, acceded to a professorship in philology at Basel, a major Swiss German-speaking university, he was expected to proceed with scholarly research within the confines of the discipline. Particular importance was attached to the first publication of a newly seated professor, doubly so in Nietzsche's case because of his youth. Philology, by this time, had lost a good deal of its initial fervor. Most available manuscripts had been cataloged and edited, and the excitement of discovery had been succeeded by increasingly narrow and myopic overspecialization. The last thing Nietzsche's sponsors in the profession wanted or expected was *The Birth of Tragedy*, which utterly abandons the very part of philology that the discipline holds most precious: its method. Worse yet, a good deal of the book's protracted attack on Socrates can be read as an insider's assault on the scientific approach to literature, rejecting it for an intuitive one.

Because Nietzsche placed the book with the same house that published Wagner's aesthetic and musicological works, *The Birth of Tragedy* was at first dismissed as an example of "literary Wagnerianism." At the time of publication, its polemical second half obscured the first, where the theory of tragedy's origin is put forth. From this reception it is possible to infer just how central the issue of Wagner was for aesthetics at the time. Wagner was a truly international figure whose influence extended well beyond the Germanic world, exercising a powerful impact not only on music but also on French, English, and Italian poetry and drama. His exile after the Revolution of 1848 became for a time an emblem of the artist's disenfranchisement in a rapidly changing Europe. Only the exile of Victor Hugo from France would have a comparable significance. The 1861 Paris premiere of *Tannhäuser* provoked the most famous riot in operatic history and led to a fashionable espousal of Wagnerian principles by Symbolist poets, including Baudelaire and Verlaine. It seemed that every artist and critic had to be clearly for or against Wagner; no middle ground was available. This is why the mere implication of Wagnerianism was sufficient to isolate Nietzsche from the academic mainstream. Wagner himself was entirely aware of this, which is why he had hoped that *The Birth of Tragedy* would find a more neutral publisher, one less associated with the Master and his cause.

Naturally, Wagner himself praised the book in no uncertain terms. In a letter to Nietzsche (as translated by Caroline V. Kerr), he wrote:

Dear Friend!

I have never read anything more beautiful than your book!

It is simply glorious! I am writing in great haste, as my excitement is so great at the moment that I must await the return of reason before being able to read it *carefully*. I have just said to Cosima that you stand second only to her, then. . . . Consider well what she has written [in ensuing letters], but cultivate indifference as far as the rest of the world is concerned!

Adieu! Run over at the first opportunity and we shall have a veritable Dionysian feast!

Yours, R. W.

Plainly, Wagner, for all his enthusiasm, foresaw what "the rest of the world" would say: that this was merely a partisan tract whose only aim was to promote Wagner's career. In fact, Wagner himself took it for granted that this was the case and saw in Nietzsche not so much an independent thinker of great promise as a powerfully eloquent ally. Eventually, this patronizing attitude on Wagner's part led to Nietzsche's disillusionment with the composer and to the break between them, which proved to be the turning point in Nietzsche's intellectual maturation. At the time, however, it apparently took Nietzsche a scant three weeks to show up at the Wagners' for the promised "Dionysian feast."

Nietzsche, meanwhile, was not unprepared for what would follow. He had already solicited and secured the services of his close friend Erwin Rohde, as both favorable reviewer and publicist. Given the older Nietzsche's complete failure to promote his work, it is interesting to see that in 1872 he went about plotting the game of literary notices with considerable canniness. He apparently realized that an author, then as now, has less to fear from bad press than from no press at all. Rohde was therefore asked to play offense and defense simultaneously.

Rohde ran into immediate trouble. He was unable to find a journal willing to publish his first effort, and sometime in February he started a second one. Meanwhile, there was no discernible reaction whatever from philologists, even Nietzsche's former teacher Ritschl, who had to be prodded before he produced a muted and noncommittal letter to his former star pupil. Rohde's review was published in May, only a few days before the expected violent reaction from philology came at last.

The reaction took the form of an article called "Philosophy of the Future! A Reply to Friedrich Nietzsche's *Birth of Tragedy.*" Its author was even younger than Nietzsche, also an alumnus of Pforta, and it was *his* first publication. His name was Ulrich von Wilamowitz-Moellendorff (1848–1931), and he would become, in his long and productive career, the leading philologist of his late day. He was ambitious in his own right, but much more committed to the standard orthodoxies of his field; his savage demolition of *The Birth of Tragedy* smacks of partisanship and a touch of jealousy, and is generally held to do him little credit. It attacks Nietzsche's style, method, and failure to use evidence, and concludes with the suggestion that Nietzsche vacate his professorial post. Wagner himself defended Nietzsche in a periodical called the *Norddeutsche allgemeine Zeitung,* the same journal that had printed Rohde's review the previous month. Rohde fired the next shot with a pamphlet called *Pseudophilology* attacking Wilamowitz, [handwritten: *After philologie = "anus philology"*] and Wilamowitz in turn produced a second part of "Philosophy of the Future" early in 1873. And so it went: a war among very young scholars too involved emotionally in their polemics to generate any genuine criticism. Because the principals were acquainted with one another, their tendency to sink to ad hominem argumentation was pronounced and unfortunate.

More damaging, probably, was the cloakroom gossip of more established philologists, who hoped to ostracize Nietzsche completely. They were apparently successful, at least for a while. Nietzsche's enrollments at Basel dropped during the fall semester, although they recovered well before his departure four years later. In any case, it was Nietzsche's health, and not his professional standing, that ended his career. Given the direction that his work took after *The Birth of Tragedy,* it is reasonable to conjecture that he would have left the university anyway. However bruising the battle of reviewers may have been, this book nonetheless sold better than any Nietzsche was to produce subsequently, aided no doubt by the very furor it aroused.

Late in his career, Nietzsche wrote about *The Birth of Tragedy* not once but twice. In 1886 he produced for a new edition a preface entitled "Versuch einer Selbstkritik," or "Attempt at Self-Criticism." Here the philosopher, in mature voice, reviews his first book according to his concerns of that time, the period when he published *Beyond Good and Evil* ("What, seen in the perspective of *life,* is the significance of morality?"). He finds it "an impossible book," "badly written, ponderous, embarrassing, image-mad and image-confused, sentimental, in places saccharine to the point of effeminacy, uneven in tempo, without the will to logical cleanliness, very convinced and therefore disdainful of proof," and on and on. Still, he declines to revise it and credits it at least with posing the problem of the Dionysian: "the problem that there *is* a problem here."

He now sees the volume as an investigation of the significance of pessimism. "Is pessimism *necessarily* a sign of decline, decay, degeneration, weary and weak instincts—as it once was in India and now is, to all appearances, among us, 'modern' men and Europeans? Is there a pessimism of *strength*?" Dionysus may be a god of madness, but "are there perhaps—a question for psychiatrists—neuroses of *health*?" And mightn't the optimism of Socratic positivism be a mask of weakness? Isn't the hunger for logic symptomatic of "dissolution and weakness?" He finds that in *The Birth of Tragedy* "perhaps for the first time, a pessimism 'beyond good and evil' is suggested." That art and not morality is the focus of the book bothers him; he finds its aesthetic foundation too limited. He also regrets that he "spoiled Dionysian premonitions with Schopenhauerian formulations."

He expresses disdain that he once could have placed so much hope in "the German spirit" and its new Empire, a *Reich* that became only "a leveling mediocrity, democracy." He sneers (somewhat benignly) at his youthful romanticism and at the humorlessness of the book: "you ought to learn to laugh, my young friends, if you are hell-bent on remaining pessimists." The preface closes with a passage from *Thus Spoke Zarathustra* on the holiness of laughter. It is, finally, a harsh but covertly affectionate portrait of his first work.

In *Ecce Homo,* one of Nietzsche's last volumes, he takes a long backward glance over his career, making a brief assessment of each of his books. Despite the notorious egomania of this attempt at intellectual autobiography, a self-absorption that some of his critics have seen as symptomatic of the advent of his final illness, Nietzsche is still as acute as ever. He reiterates his regret at "the cadaverous perfume of Schopenhauer"[1] in *The Birth of Tragedy* and recalls once more the Franco-Prussian War and the heat of that hopeful moment. But now his main misgivings stem from the book's Wagnerianism and from the fact that the antithesis of Apollo and Dionysus did not really succeed in escaping Hegelian dialectical logic. He does congratulate himself on the discovery of the Dionysian and with being the first to see "morality itself as a symptom of decadence." He finds that the book points the way to a deeper understanding than that of "wretched and shallow chatter about optimism versus pessimism," tending toward "a

Yes-saying without reservation, even to suffering, even to guilt, even to everything that is questionable and strange in existence" (272).

"In this sense I have the right to understand myself as the first *tragic philosopher*—that is, the most extreme opposite and antipode of a pessimistic philosopher" (273). Tragedy by now has for Nietzsche a very specific meaning: the ability to affirm even "passing away *and destroying*"—that is, affirming even negation. "A tremendous hope speaks out of this essay. In the end I lack all reason to renounce the hope for a Dionysian future of music. . . . Wagner, Bayreuth, the whole wretched German pettiness are a cloud in which an infinite mirage of the future is reflected" (274).

Since Nietzsche's death, *The Birth of Tragedy* has risen and fallen in critical estimation along with the rest of his work. Despite its particular interest for theorists of tragedy, it is very much part of Nietzsche's oeuvre and has rightly been treated as such (as it is by the author himself). Eventually even later philologists accepted it for what it is: Eduard Fraenkel, dean of the field after Wilamowitz and a student of that antagonist of Nietzsche, paid it warm tributes. More speculative modern classical scholars, from Gilbert Murray to the Texas classicists of the 1960s, placed it among the most influential texts in their field. For all the book's flaws, many acknowledged by the author in later years, and for all the righteous resistance it encountered from the contemporary academic world, it has outlasted its initial reception to find a permanent place in the literature of speculative thought.

4

A BRIEF GLOSSARY

For all its interdisciplinary appeal, *The Birth of Tragedy* is a philosophical work, and therefore quite impossible to discuss without using philosophical terminology. This is true even in an introductory commentary like the present one. I am referring not to jargon, but to technical vocabulary born of necessity, much like other specialized lexicons in fields such as automobile repair, chess, dentistry, and physics. To ease the reader's way through the more philosophical portions of the commentary, I am including the following very brief, informal glossary, with the warning that each of the entries is guilty of almost preposterous oversimplification.

ANTINOMIES: Pairs of logical oppositions.

DIALECTICS: Reasoning by opposition.

EPISTEMOLOGY: The branch of Metaphysics (q.v.) concerned with Knowing.

IDEALISM: Any philosophical system that asserts the priority of mind over matter; the belief that consciousness, rather than the material world, is the "real reality." The opposite of Materialism (q.v.).

MATERIALISM: Any philosophical system that asserts the priority of matter over mind. The opposite of Idealism (q.v.).

Metaphysics: The science of being and knowing. The term means *after/beyond ~~with~~ physics," indicating that metaphysics investigates the underlying principles of reality.

Noumena: All things that lie beyond the reach of the senses. Since we cannot say where the Phenomena (q.v.) come from, it may be hypothesized that there is a material or even conscious substratum lying "behind" sense impressions that may be somehow connected to their transmission—or may not be. See Thing-in-Itself.

Object: What is perceived. See Subject.

Ontology: The branch of Metaphysics (q.v.) that deals with Being.

Phenomena: Units of sensory perception. The phenomenal realm is therefore the world of the senses. See Noumena.

Representation: In Schopenhauer, sense impressions as ordered by the perceiving consciousness.

Subject: The perceiver. See Object.

Syllogism: A diagram of a logical argument, usually consisting of two premises and a conclusion.

Thesis, Antithesis, Synthesis: In a Hegelian syllogism, a proposition, its logical opposite, and the mediation between them.

Thing-in-Itself: The object as it exists absolutely, beyond perception. See Noumena.

Will: In Schopenhauer, a noumenal force that causes us to desire involvement with the world of representations (q.v.).

A
Reading

5

THE
BIRTH OF TRAGEDY

Section 1

APOLLO AND DIONYSUS

The history of Western consciousness is the history of dialectical thought. In other words, the mixture of Greco-Roman and Hebraic elements that make up our culture tend by tradition to cause us to think in oppositions. We laugh when a child says that chocolate and vanilla are opposites, but adults are often guilty of equally unexamined antitheses. Some think of the black and white races as opposite, and almost everyone thinks that way about the two sexes. But are the sexes really opposite, or are they merely complementary biological types? Are the races opposed, or are they merely varieties of human beings deposited side by side on earth?

The tendency to think dialectically goes back to the Greek pre-Socratic philosophers of the late sixth century B.C.—that is, nearly to the beginning of recorded thought—when the astronomer-mathematician-musicologist Pythagoras believed that the universe is composed of atoms held in harmony by forces at once geometrical and theological. Probably under his influence, Heraclitus, an Ionian of the early fifth century B.C., suggested that the cohesion of the universe depends upon the unity of opposites. Zeno the Eleatic, a later fifth-century thinker, is said to have developed dialectics into a *method*, or way of thinking philosophically.

Credit for bringing this method to the center of philosophy is universally given to Socrates, at least as he appears in the *Dialogues* of Plato. In these conversations between Socrates and a series of antagonists, the philosopher attempts to open new avenues of investigation by entertaining, provisionally, the *opposite* of what is commonly believed about any given subject. This procedure, curiously enough, is followed in the interest of logical consistency. Socrates' aim is to elicit from his adversaries truths that they already know, but do not know they know.

Socrates left no writings of his own; we know him only through Plato and Xenophon. The historical Socrates is therefore less important than the literary character of the same name. In *The Birth of Tragedy*, Socrates is a character once again, only this time he is not a hero as in Plato, but a kind of villain.

The reason for rehearsing the history of dialectics at the start of this commentary is that we must first come to some sort of understanding about the relationship of Dionysus and Apollo, who are introduced in the opening paragraph of Nietzsche's book. It would be easy to see them as *opposites*, and indeed as Nietzsche develops them they do have certain opposing characteristics. He even calls them opposites in the opening sentence of the second section. They are not, however, antitheses who hold some interpolated logical truth between them, or who are merely extremes to be regulated into some kind of golden mean. To see what they are, we will have to look briefly at the intellectual background against which *The Birth of Tragedy* was composed.

Nietzsche's career as a philosopher began at the twilight of a century-old heyday of German dialectical thought. Immanuel Kant, the founder of modern philosophy (that is, philosophy that believes in truth outside of God), developed a series of antinomies as part of his metaphysics, but they seem incidental in his work, compared with the central place given to dialectics by ensuing philosophers such as Schelling (1775–1854), Fichte (1762–1879), and particularly G. W. F. Hegel (1770–1831). Hegel thought that consciousness itself is the whole of reality, and he believed it to be created and enhanced by a process of opposition. His writings on logic form the basis for his metaphysics, aesthetics, ethics, and philosophy of history. According to his scheme, consciousness moves across logical "time" by an interconnected chain of syllogisms. An initial proposition, called a thesis, immediately generates its own opposite, the antithesis. Between these two, a logical middle ground is created; this is called the synthesis. Each synthesis then becomes a new thesis, and the process continues. This is Hegel's equivalent of Genesis, from which he claims that all thought, feeling, history—all human consciousness—originates.

Hegal's influence was enormous. He spawned another generation of dialectical thinkers, among them Karl Marx. The presence of Hegelian thought would have been inescapable for the young Nietzsche, but from the start he seems to have been more attracted by the work of another less rigorously dialectical philosopher, though a dialectician nonetheless, Arthur Schopenhauer (1788–1860). Schopenhauer's shadow is very dark across the pages of *The Birth of Tragedy,* as Nietzsche acknowledges in a late preface he wrote in 1886. Before discussing this influence, however, let us finish with the matter of dialectics and how it affects our understanding of Apollo and Dionysus.

One of the major undertakings of Nietzsche's later philosophical career is a critique of dialectics, an investigation of why it is that Westerners are so addicted to thinking in oppositions. In time Nietzsche decides that the whole apparatus of dialectical thought, all the way back to Plato, needs to be dismantled if philosophy is to come any closer to understanding consciousness. What Nietzsche finds most questionable, in the long run, is the assumption that between the poles of an opposition lies some *logical* truth. Formal logic is for Nietzsche a mere game constructed more out of the love of order than the desire to further knowledge. He doubts the synthesis, then, above all. Despite the fact that *The Birth of Tragedy* is an early book, and despite the fact that it was written under the spell of the Schopenhauerian (and maybe also the Hegelian) dialectic, it would be wrong to see the "duality" (*Duplizitat*) of Apollo and Dionysus as a dialectical opposition in the logical sense. Nietzsche makes no promise that any logical synthesis lies in the reconciliation of the two gods. Far from it. It is in part to discredit this proposition that Socrates is introduced as an antagonist, a proponent of the destructive falsity of logic in general, and implicitly of dialectics in particular.

So how *are* we to understand Apollo and Dionysus? Not logically, for logic as an exclusive criterion is repudiated in the very first sentence of *The Birth of Tragedy*, to be supplanted by "unmittelbaren Sicherheit der Anschauung"—"immediate certainty of vision," as Kaufmann translates it, but also "unmiddleable" or "unmediated" certainty: that is, not the logical certainty of a dialectical synthesis. The modes of the two gods are immediately compared with those of the two sexes—both are required, but despite their "perpetual strife" they are *not* logical opposites. To emphasize this crucial point, Nietzsche goes on, still in his first paragraph, to claim that the Greeks, who created these "art deities," used gods instead of concepts (logical units) in their thinking. So that even as he is introducing his terminology, Nietzsche is already making a statement about the method he will use: it will rely on immediate vision rather than logic. Given the fact that *The Birth of Tragedy* is the author's first book, it is possible in retrospect to see this passage as an announcement of Nietzsche's work as a whole.

Trained not as a philosopher but as a philologist, Nietzsche might have been expected to practice some form of systematic thought, likely dialectical thought, in his first major published work. Instead, he introduces a sort of "anti-dialectic" in Apollo and Dionysus, and in the same breath renounces logic in favor of vision. Given the formality of German academia in the nineteenth century, it is not difficult to see why *The Birth of Tragedy* created shock waves from its very first words.

· · ·

A Reading

Who are these "art deities of the Greeks," Apollo and Dionysus?

Apollo is a sun-god, a mainstay of the Olympian pantheon, a son of Zeus begotten upon a mortal woman named Leto. The Romans later made him the charioteer who drives the sun's horses across the sky each day, conflating him with Helios, another Greek sun-god. For the Greeks, however, Apollo's association with the sun is less mechanical than Helios's, more closely connected with the healing properties of light. Apollo the healer could also destroy, often through disease. His identification with the arts is strong. He reigns over the Muses and plays the lyre, and he is therefore closely associated with both music and poetry (since the recitation of poetry in ancient Greece was ordinarily accompanied by a stringed instrument). In addition, Nietzsche, right from the start of *The Birth of Tragedy,* connects him with sculpture as well.

Dionysus is also a son of Zeus, begotten upon a mortal woman named Semele. Despite the fact that this makes Apollo and Dionysus half-brothers, Dionysus is actually a later entry into the ranks of Greek gods, lacking Apollo's almost aboriginal seniority. Dionysus, Nietzsche will argue, is a Hellenized Asiatic god, possibly derived from Egyptian seasonal divinities like Osirus. It is said that Semele asked her disguised Olympian lover to reveal his true identity. Zeus refused, but she insisted. When he manifested his thunderbolt as proof of who he was, she died from it. Hermes rescued the fetus and made a long incision in Zeus's thigh, into which the baby was inserted. There it completed its gestation—so that in effect Zeus became Dionysus's mother as well as his father.

Later commentators, working under the influence of *The Birth of Tragedy,* claim that this story is late and rather ad hoc. George Thomson in particular argues that the legalization of the Dionysian religion after Peisistratos's sixth-century B.C. coup d'état necessitated some sort of story to justify adding the upstart god to the original pantheon. Whether this is the case or not, it is clear that Dionysus is a later god, produced as much by social circumstances as by theological development.

Dionysus is above all an agrarian god. He is ritually dismembered in the fall and reborn in the spring, an emblematic divinity embodying human dependency upon the seasons, especially among farmers, whose livelihood is made or broken by these natural cycles. The vegetable world upon which agriculture depends dies in the fall and is reborn in the spring; so does Dionysus. The god then comes to be associated with the mysterious power that revives growth after the deadness of winter. Dionysus may be something like what Dylan Thomas called "the force that through the green fuse drives the flower."[2]

Thomson, in *Aeschylus and Athens,* gives a continuation of the myth of the young god's birth from the thigh of Zeus: "Enraged at the honors which Zeus was bestowing on the child, Hera suborned the Titans and persuaded them to destroy it. Accordingly, having provided themselves with attractive toys . . . the Titans enticed the child from the Kouretes, in whose charge it had been placed, tore it in pieces, threw the limbs into a cauldron and boiled and ate them. . . . When Zeus discovered what had happened, he blasted the Titans with his thunderbolt, and in some way . . . the dead child was brought to life again."[3] The notion of a god whose birth and death are both cause for celebration was of course borrowed by Christianity, which put the birth of the god in the winter and conflated his death and rebirth into a single event in the spring.

Dionysus, like Apollo, has a strong identification with art. While Apollo plays stringed instruments, Dionysus (sometime as his aspect Pan) is usually seen playing wind instruments—another connection with rural life, since a shepherd or someone working in the fields cannot, for obvious reasons, take along a lyre, while they might slip a small flute easily into a pocket or behind a belt. Dionysus's association with dance, of which Nietzsche will make a great deal, may go back to the early ritual worship of the god, long before the religion was legalized in Athens. In antiquity, orgiastic dancing was always associated with the early cults, along with occasional unsubstantiated rumors of human sacrifice and sexual extravagance.

Notice that Apollo and Dionysus, although they may possess some antithetical characteristics, are not opposites any more than stringed and wind instruments are. Or any more than the two sexes. It is from their "coupling" (*Paarung*) that tragedy is generated.

PHILOSOPHICAL BACKGROUND

Presenting the contrast (*Gegensatz*) between the gods, still careful to avoid all hint of *logical* opposition, Nietzsche links Apollo with dreams and Dionysus with intoxication, two very different physiological states, although not dialectically opposed. The ensuing five paragraphs on Apollo are heavily tinged with the tone and terminology of Schopenhauer. Nietzsche makes no attempt to disguise this, citing the earlier philosopher for corroboration as he will do frequently throughout his text.

Schopenhauer was the reigning influence on Nietzsche's early development as a thinker. Like Nietzsche, Schopenhauer was something of a prodigy, publishing his first philosophical work, *On The Fourfold Root of the Principle of Sufficient Reason,* in 1813 when he was about twenty-five years old. This treatise is in fact his doctoral dissertation, and it contains a critique of the thought of Immanuel Kant (1724–1804) that carries over into Schopenhauer's main work, the basis of his whole philosophical system, *Die Welt als Wille und Vorstellung* (1819), usually translated as *The World as Will and Representation.* In order to understand this work and its influence on Nietzsche, we must backtrack still further and make a brief account of Kant and his influence.

In the philosophy of the Middle Ages and the Renaissance, it is assumed that the reality of the world stems from God. God not only established reality at the time of the creation; he also underwrites its continuation by in effect *re-creating* the world at every moment. From Saint Augustine to the generation of philosophers just prior to Kant— for example, the Irish Bishop George Berkeley (1685–1753)—the notion that God determines what is real is never much questioned. As the eighteenth century progressed, however, this theocentric view of the world began to come apart. From a social standpoint, it was seen as part of the cultural apparatus that kept the aristocracy in power, while the rising middle class was beginning to act to take power for itself. The American Revolution (1776) and the French Revolution (1789), apart from their importance as political events, were ideological events as well. They served to reinforce the notion that the human species has an integrity all its own, an ability to determine reality apart from God.

The most radical philosophical challenge to the old theocentrism came from empiricism, particularly the work of John Locke (1632–1704), whose *Essay Concerning Human Understanding* (1690) launched the first attack on the notion of innate (i.e., God-given) ideas. Locke believes that perception, and the way perception is received and ordered by the human mind, is responsible for the generation of our ideas. David Hume (1711–76), a Scottish philosopher, economist, and historian, extended and developed Locke's empiricism. An avowed atheist, Hume tries to find a way to reassign from God to humanity the authority to declare an object or an experience real. While many of his arguments for the integrity of perception are persuasive, Hume runs aground on the problem of predictability and the continuity of experience.

The problem is this: let us assume for the moment that we can trust our senses and that our brains are capable of making basic judgments about reality without the intercession of God. Empiricism argues that we make such judgments not from innate ideas or abstract principles, but from our inductive observation of the world. Hence we may say "All cows have four feet" on the basis of our repeated observation of cows. The trouble is that there is no way we can be sure that the very next cow we see will not have five feet. No matter how many thousands of cows we observe, there is always the possibility that the next one will be different.

Another example makes this dilemma even more painful. We say, "The sun comes up in the morning." But how can we be sure that the sun will come up again tomorrow morning, as it has in the past? In other words, how can we be sure that the future will provide continuity with the past? We can say, to be sure, that "In the past, the sun has always come up the next morning," or, "In the past, the future was always like the past," but this is plainly a self-annihilating argument, a reductio ad absurdam. Hume, in despair of finding an irrefutable logical basis for his empirical position, proposed *habit* as the principle that enables humanity to live from day to day with certainty.

Kant was deeply impressed with Hume's work, particularly the *Enquiry Concerning Human Understanding* (1748). Kant said this work woke him from his "dogmatic slumber," but he saw that Hume's last-minute reliance on so flimsy a concept as habit is insufficient grounds for transferring epistemological authority from God to humanity. Unlike Schopenhauer and Nietzsche, Kant was no prodigy, publishing *The Critique of Pure Reason,* his first significant work, in 1781, when he was already in his late fifties.

Kant's first critique argues that the source of reality lies within the structure of human consciousness itself. Time and space, which he calls "forms of experience," do not lie outside the mind as properties of *things,* but are really the cognitive groundwork without which any notion of experience would be quite incomprehensible. Indeed it *is* impossible to imagine anything that could be called experience taking place outside of space and time. Then, Kant proposes a system of twelve "categories" of consciousness that in sum constitute an apparatus for the validation of experience. Kant refers to perception as a preliminary state; *experience* follows upon a process called *judgment,* which can give or deny a perception incontrovertible reality.

This sounds like quibbling at first, a kind of formalizing of Hume's "habit," but it was the most earth-shaking philosophical event of the modern world, and it remains so today—an event in philosophy on a par with the French Revolution in politics. Kant rigorously demonstrates that making human consciousness the arena for the determination of reality does not require a sacrifice of philosophical certainty and (although Kant, unlike Hume, is no atheist) does not require God's intercession.

At the close of his career, Kant felt that he had settled this question forever, but there are some distressing loopholes in his admirable system. Despite his vindication of perception as the single basis for a judgment of reality, he leaves in place, beyond the reach of perception, the *ding-an-sich* or thing-in-itself, an absolute material plane of existence whose relationship to our perceptions can never be firmly established.

An example may help to make this clear. You look at the book you are holding in your hands; you see its outlines, its color, the many glyphs on its pages. You touch it; it is solid. You probably assume that there is an actual book out there sending signals of sight and touch that your senses receive and process. But how can you be sure this is true? All you know is what your senses tell you. But what is sending the signals that your senses receive? We cannot "look behind" the sensory signals we are receiving to see what is transmitting them. The signals received by the senses are called "phenomena"; the mysterious objects (or whatever they are) that lie beyond perception are called "noumena." Even while Kant endows phenomena with a new and enormous significance as the raw material from which the brain creates experience, he retains the noumenal realm with the caution that our senses must never try to apperceive it; to try to do so, he says, would lead us into the "transcendental illusion." Reason, on the other hand, can *think about* the problem of the noumenal realm, and that process generates endeavors such as theology, ethics, aesthetics, and—of course—metaphysics itself. But the "understanding," the part of consciousness that creates and authenticates daily reality, is banned from trespassing in the noumenal realm of the thing-in-itself.

This may seem a small price to pay for the certainty and integrity Kant believed he had imparted to human consciousness. He had (like Prometheus) stolen from God a creative fire and given it to man. Humanity can believe in God if it chooses, but it can now exist in complete autonomy without fear that the fabric of the world will fall apart as a result. Yet Kant's maintenance of the noumenal realm causes his whole system to become unstable, in the eyes of many later philosophers. Most of the subsequent history of German idealism is the story of various schemes to eliminate the problem and restore stability to Kant's humanized view of reality.

It is therefore not terribly surprising that Schopenhauer begins his

A Reading

career with a critique of Kant. In order to get around the problem of the thing-in-itself, Schopenhauer asserts the fundamental interdependency of subject and object. In fact, if we stop to consider this, such an interdependency seems to be almost a semantic necessity, for what meaning could be assigned to "subject" (or perceiver) if there were nothing to be perceived? What meaning would "object" (of perception) have if there were no perceiver? This may seem a bit silly; nonetheless it allows Schopenhauer to argue (in the very first section of his great tome) that "the world is representation." That is, we all create reality for ourselves by *re-presenting* the raw material of the senses in a coherent way, and no "objective" realm of *ding-an-sich* or material substratum need be taken into account. Such hypothetical "objects" could not be objects at all, since they lie beyond the reach of subjects. To say that "the world is representation" is to assert that the internally determining consciousness that Kant proposes is valid on *all* levels.

Schopenhauer also rejects all of Kant's categories except causality. Without belaboring this historical discussion, it is necessary to say that among the rejected categories is one called reality—that is, the part of consciousness that, in Kant's hypothesis, filters out hallucinations, optical illusions, and the like, and also enables us to distinguish between waking experience and dreams. It is this Kantian category that the English poet-critic Samuel Taylor Coleridge (1772–1834) is attacking in his famous doctrine of Secondary Imagination in the *Biographia Literaria* (1817). More than any other German philosopher before Nietzsche, Schopenhauer has a special appeal for artists. This is in part because of his allowance of dreams as a valid part of consciousness. "Life and dreams," he writes in section 5 of the first part of *The World as Will and Representation*, "are leaves of one and the same book. . . . Thus, although individual dreams are marked off from real life by the fact that they do not fit into the continuity of experience that runs constantly through life, and waking up indicates this difference, yet that very continuity of experience belongs to real life as its form, and the dream can likewise point to a continuity in itself. Now if we assume a standpoint of judgment external to both, we find no distinct difference in their nature, and are forced to concede to the poets that life is a long dream."[4]

THE SCHOPENHAUERIAN GODS

The god Apollo is associated by Nietzsche with the Schopenhauerian concept of Representation, by which he meant that reality is a re-presentation of what the senses provide. Schopenhauer argues that we accomplish this representation as individuals, and in this he believes he is clarifying Kant, who saw in individual consciousness all the apparatus needed for universal judgment. Schopenhauer calls this the *principium individuationis,* a Latin phrase meaning "the principle of individuation." Nietzsche's Apollo is thus not only an embodiment of representation, but also a figure for individuation (which makes representation possible).

subject

Nietzsche (recollecting Schopenhauer's magnificent passages on dreams) associates Apollo with the dream state and quotes his fellow Schopenhauerian Richard Wagner to help establish the relationship between art and dream. Like Schopenhauer, Nietzsche thinks that "life and dreams are leaves of one and the same book." But he begins with dreams, using them as a model for "real life," which in the ensuing paragraph he finds to be "mere appearance" (*Schein*), paraphrasing Schopenhauer on "the ability to view men and things as mere phantoms or dreams."

Nietzsche's task at this point is to establish Apollo as the god of dreams and dreamlike "representation." It is not going to be easy to do, since the Greek Apollo is a sun-god and would not ordinarily be construed as the embodiment of something so nocturnal as dreams. Nietzsche in fact uses several different approaches telescoped together as if they made up a single argument. It is probably best to take these one at a time.

1. "Apollo, the god of all plastic energies, is at the same time the soothsaying god." Kaufmann's translation of "bildnerischen Kräfte" as "plastic energies" is at first glance a little self-contradictory. Some-

thing like "shaping powers" or "formal skills" might be clearer. This is a reference to the association of Apollo with sculpture that Nietzsche made earlier. The term "plastic arts" in English refers to sculpture primarily. *The Oxford English Dictionary* defines plastic art as "the art of shaping or modeling; any art in which this is done, as sculpture or ceramics." Nietzsche is asserting Apollo's creative powers, but at the same time is calling him a soothsaying (*wahrsagende*) or truth-telling god. In this context, "truth-telling" presumably indicates a willingness to recognize the dreamlike nature of what is apparently reality. In other words, Nietzsche acknowledges the conventional view of Apollo as a molder of material things, while also asserting the god's awareness of the provisional nature of material reality.

2. The next argument is based on the root (*Wurzel*) of Apollo's name, which Nietzsche asserts is "the shining one." Kaufmann's footnote explains the German play on the word *Schein* ("appearance"). Nietzsche may have some conventional Greek epithet for Apollo in mind; certainly a sun-god could well be referred to as "the shining one." If so, it would be better if he gave us the specific epithet he has in mind, for the source of Apollo's name is actually the Greek verb meaning "to destroy."

3. The sun-god, god of light, shines over the inner fantasy-world. Accordingly, the Apollo who heals the "everyday world" with light becomes, in the inner world, a soothsayer and an artist, who, Nietzsche asserts, are themselves healers. As part of that healing power, the god must manifest "measured restraint" and "the calm of the sculptor god."

4. The quotation from Schopenhauer and the ensuing sentence conclude the introductory passage on Apollo. Schopenhauer's depiction of the individual as a sailor on stormy seas resembles Richard Wagner's musicological conception of singers' voices as ships floating upon the sea of the orchestra. The image of a calm individual weathering a choatic world is a vivid one and gives a clear sense of what Nietzsche intends Apollo to stand for.

All in all, these four points do not cohere particularly well. Nietzsche tends to avoid "logical" argumentation; this becomes increasingly true in his maturity as a writer. What must be gleaned from the haphazard continuity of this passage is that the Greek god Apollo is being revalued and that Nietzsche's Apollo will not, in the long run, be much like the original. Yet Nietzsche feels compelled to try, however unsuccessfully, to make the alignment between his Apollo and the Greek one, possibly because *The Birth of Tragedy* was after all presented as a tract in classical philology.

· · ·

What does Nietzsche have Apollo dreaming about? The cool, collected, highly individuated god, dreaming sculptures into being, standing high above the chaos, is not so much dreaming as recognizing that the world is a dream. Apollo is the Schopenhauerian god of representation. Plainly the Greek divinity has been left behind in this revaluation.

The connection of Dionysus with intoxication is far less forced than that of Apollo with dreams. In Greek myth, Dionysus was traditionally associated with wine, and one of his most common aspects is Bacchus, the god of the grape. It is similarly unforced for Nietzsche to identify Dionysus with the collapse of the *principium individuationis*. Something of that sort seems to be going on in Euripides' play *The Bacchae*, which pits Dionysus against an arrogant and self-centered young king, Pentheus. The delight that Dionysus takes in bringing about the downfall of Pentheus makes one wonder if the title "the destroyer" (which Nietzsche seems anxious to remove quietly from Apollo) might fit Dionysus better. For it is nothing less than "blissful ecstasy" (*wonnevolle Verzückung*) that the god feels "at this collapse of the *principium individuationis*."

In the following paragraph, Nietzsche expands upon the idea of intoxication. It may be the "narcotic draught" or the coming of spring—something already sacred to the original Dionysus. The updating process begins at once, as Nietzsche brings Dionysian esctasies into the German Middle Ages, and, implicitly, into the present. Shortly, even Beethoven's "Ode to Joy" will be said to embody Dionysus.

A Reading

"The union between man and man" is reaffirmed; that is, Dionysus is a collective divinity even as Apollo is an individuated one. Social barriers are broken down. "Now the slave is a free man." The veil of *Maya* (which Nietzsche associates with the illusionary Schopenhauerian "representation") is "now merely fluttering in tatters." Plainly, Dionysus emblematizes something of a philosophical nature, just as Apollo did. And once again, it is something from Schopenhauer.

If Apollo is identified with representation, Dionysus is identified with the Will, the other major element in Schopenhauer's philosophical system. The relationship of Will and representation, as Schopenhauer develops it in the second section of *The World as Will and Representation,* is really a version of what is called in philosophy "the mind-body problem." The perceptions that comprise the raw material for representation are already past their physical inputs before consciousness organizes them. In other words, the physical media of perception are of no inherent interest insofar as representation is concerned. But what about the body? Is it to be divorced so completely from the mind?

"The action of the body is nothing but the act of Will objectified," wrote Schopenhauer in the eighteenth section of his work. Even more explicitly, a couple of sentences later he writes "that the whole body is nothing but the objectified will, i.e., the will that has become representation."[5] This means that through the mind's perception of the body, consciousness gains access to the Will, and can begin to think about it. But what is this Will? Schopenhauer speaks of it first as a manifestation of change, then of the desire for change. In the fourth book of *The World as Will and Representation* he explicitly identifies it with "the will to live." Plainly he sees it as the appetitive faculty that causes consciousness (which otherwise treats the "represented" world as dreamlike) to want to engage itself with the world. It is thus a kind of primordial life force. But to understand Schopenhauer's ambivalence on the subject, we need once again to delve briefly into the history of the problem.

When Kant relocated the mechanism for establishing reality

from God to the human mind, he necessarily implied that there was something divine in human consciousness. Those who, for the reasons discussed above, found Kant's system unsatisfactory, sought to invent new schemata that would make plainer the way in which human awareness could be a replacement for divinity. Hegel turns Kant's system inside out, removing the universalizing consciousness from the individual mind and giving it an objective, externalized form. This he calls the Absolute. The Absolute is the sum of all human awareness and experience—every thought ever held, every sensation ever felt, every bit of knowledge and emotion that have composed the totality of human history. Yet the Absolute is transcendental, greater than the sum of its parts. It grows as human experience expands and history continues. Envisioned as a giant mind enveloping the planet, it is closer to a god than the forms and categories of Kant could ever be. In the hands of the American Ralph Waldo Emerson (who greatly influenced Nietzsche), it is renamed the Oversoul and is experienced as a pantheistic power that informs all nature, particularly human nature.

This surrogate god of the modern age is positivistic in that it manifests progress—an ever-growing consciousness that will continue to expand until it reaches the *An-Sich-Für-Sich,* or complete self-fulfillment. At this time history will end, and Being will succeed Becoming as the mode of all existence. Hegel regards this as a most optimistic prospect, since it provides a hopeful eschatology for human life. Schopenhauer, on the other hand, is a pessimist. Although he and Hegel share the influence of Hinduism (hence the persistence of the term *Maya* in the first section of *The Birth of Tragedy*), Hegel interprets that Eastern religion as a corroboration of his Absolute spirit, whereas Schopenhauer sees it as a vindication of his own skepticism about the phenomenal realm.

Emerging from the same Kantian background, Schopenhauer (who, as if to emphasize the conflict, once scheduled his lectures at the same hour as Hegel's, then complained when no one came) shares with Hegel a mistrust of Kant's claim that the universal can be reached by way of the individual. So Schopenhauer develops his own version of the Absolute—except it is not good, but evil. This is the Will. It is the force that brings change; but change is rarely, and only temporarily, for the better. Instead of absorbing individual effort into a constructive and collective history, like the Absolute, the Will seduces individuals to believe that the world may be real, not just the source of suspect representations. Eventually, Schopenhauer comes to urge humanity to turn away from the Will and the world, and away from the body, since it is the Will's objectification. He urges resignation instead of desire. In his own theory of tragedy, in section 51 of *The World as Will and Representation,* Schopenhauer suggests that the *hamartia,* or "flaw," of all tragic protagonists lies in their engagement with the Will, which brings in its wake "the guilt of existence itself."

To escape that guilt, one ought not to engage with the Will at all. Instead, one should cultivate a kind of resignation, a turning away from an appetitive life that can only end in grief and disappointment. To engage with the world on the terms dictated by the Will, then, is for Schopenhauer the essence of tragedy, and therefore all tragic drama is to be read as a kind of allegory. What happens to tragic heroes can happen to us all:

> It is one and the same Will, living and appearing in them all, whose phenomena fight with one another and tear one another to pieces. . . . Here and there it reaches thoughtfulness and is softened more or less by the light of knowledge, until at last in the individual case this knowledge is purified and enhanced by suffering itself. It then reaches the point where the phenomenon, the veil of Maya, no longer deceives it. It sees through the form of the phenomenon, the *principium individuationis;* the egotism resting on this expires with it.[6]

The problem of the Will was to preoccupy Nietzsche for all of his career. The posthumous fragments collected by his sister are published under the title *Die Wille zur Macht* (*The Will To Power*). At this stage of his career, however, Nietzsche seems principally preoccupied with liberating the concept of the Will from Schopenhauerian pessimism. To put it a bit too baldly, Nietzsche does not take the Schopenhauerian position that the Will and the body that manifests it *must* be evil. He wants to find a means to vindicate the ability to be intoxicated with the world, however false the world may prove to be. And the means for this vindication he calls Dionysus.

In the final paragraph of the first section, Nietzsche dwells upon dancing, in which the body itself becomes a work of art. He quickly delineates those characteristics of Dionysus that he finds most valuable: the god's transindividual or collective nature; his ability to forge art out of the very objects of the Will; and his intoxication, the ecstasy that no longer doubts the fragile Apollinian representations that are called the veil of *Maya*.

Section 2

The Apollinian and the Dionysian are "artistic energies which burst forth from nature herself, *without the mediation of the human artist.*" The idea of art occurring in nature, prior to the artist, is a formulation that threatens the very definitions of art and of nature. We tend to use "art" to designate forms of order that result from human design, whereas "nature" ordinarily denotes all of reality that occurs outside of human contrivance. (This is true, by the way, even of the phrase "human nature," which designates elements in the character of our species over which we have no direct control.) And so to assert that nature has "art impulses" seems at first glance to be a semantic absurdity.

Nietzsche designates two natural states of consciousness, dreams on the one hand and intoxication (*Trunkenheit*—drunkenness, not necessarily limited to the alcoholic sense) on the other, each of which has a special relationship to the "imitation" the artist engages in. With reference to these archetypal art-states, the human artist is necessarily

A Reading

Nachahmer—a copier, counterfeiter, imitator. Artists and, in some instances, whole genres may be classified according to which of the two natural states they choose as the primary object of imitation. The human artist imitates either the Apollinian dream state, or the Dionysian intoxication, or—in the case of the tragic artist—both at once. Dreams and intoxication are *Kunsttreibe*, or natural powers driving art. Their existence would argue for a source of art that precedes any human contrivance. This is what Apollo and Dionysus signify. They are gods, hence they are part nature and part something else. Similarly, art is a direct outgrowth of nature and not merely a human embellishment upon it.

By making the natural existence of art an axiom, bypassing either recapitulation or rebuttal of any previous thought on the matter, Nietzsche is walking quickly and lightly over a minefield. The question of distinguishing natural from human-made beauty is of concern to almost all of his philosophical predecessors. The word *aesthetic* comes from the Greek verb meaning "to perceive." This tells us that the issue is an intimate part of all metaphysics. Nietzsche is often rightly faulted for his habit of taking something debatable and positing it as an axiom, and this brief passage is a good example. Its role in the book's argument is to establish Nietzsche's belief in the primal importance of art, that art is as fundamental as the gods, or as nature itself. There will be many later portions of the text that depend upon this assertion. Still, it is easy to see why Nietzsche's method is so controversial. He neither argues the point philosophically, nor documents it historically, nor proves it logically. It is a given.

What follows is a direct confrontation with Aristotle, whose *Poetics*, both in Nietzsche's time and our own, is the one unavoidable text in the field of theory of tragedy. This is true not because its conclusions are infallible; on the contrary, the *Poetics* is a bit of a mess, a posthumous work stitched together by Aristotle's students from lecture notes. What makes Aristotle indispensable is that he created a terminology for discussing tragedy and, in so doing, shaped the very universe of discourse within which all subsequent discussions of tragedy have taken place. Of all modern theorists of tragedy,

Nietzsche strays farthest from Aristotle's vocabulary. It is for this reason appropriate that Nietzsche (deliberately?) misquotes the *Poetics* in this rare direct allusion to it.

Aristotle nowhere says flatly that art (poetry, specifically) is the imitation *of nature*. He implies, in the opening passages of the *Poetics*, that all art is imitation (mimesis), but he sees it as imitating *human* events, *human* character, *human* action—human nature, perhaps, but not nature in the general sense. Nietzsche is in effect enlisting Aristotle's support for his idea of prehuman "art impulses" occurring naturally. But certainly Aristotle does not express the idea that art imitates some kind of "natural art" or that art imitates dreams and/or intoxications.

To begin to explicate what he means by Apollo, Nietzsche speaks of Greek dreams as if they were inherently works of art, bas-reliefs, or the epics of Homer. This is utterly conjectural, of course. Imagine pretending to know what dreams were like in antiquity! There is something admirable, even breathtaking, in Nietzsche's tone of absolute confidence as he makes such startling leaps. Even putting the impossibility of any "proof" aside, there is a circularity to the statement. For it is from the study of Greek art that Nietzsche forms his ideas of Greek dreams—which he then says are responsible somehow for Greek art, "dreaming Greeks as Homers and Homer as a dreaming Greek." This may be as dubious as the ontological argument for the existence of God, which claims that the idea of God can only come from God and that therefore, since we have that idea, God must exist.

There is a kind of trompe l'oeil going on here, yet it is a vivid one, creating the illusion that Nietzsche is somehow privy to a sort of archaeology of consciousness itself and is exhuming an earlier structure to explain the present one. Throughout Nietzsche's career, he exhibits many such flagrant but intuitively persuasive flauntings of logic; one of the problems with an early work like *The Birth of Tragedy* is that the methodological difficulties of such an attack are not yet solved. No doubt aware that his resistance to logic places him in conflict with the academic audience to whom he has to address his first book, he cannot yet develop his intuitive style as freely as he will be able to later. In fact, Nietzsche will reach his fullest voice, alas, only when he has no audience left at all.

With Dionysus, he claims to find himself on less conjectural ground. Here he introduces the idea that Dionysian rituals were imported into Greece from other parts of the ancient world and came rather late into the domain of a disdaining Olympian Apollo. It is this hypothesis that is responsible for much of the subsequent scholarly interest in *The Birth of Tragedy*. Nietzsche presents his account of the nature and origin of Dionysian ritual as if it were an incontrovertible historical fact. Despite some disjointed and cursory examples (such as the Babylonian Sacaca), the absence of footnotes and hard fact here is particularly difficult. Subsequent anthropological theorists, such as Gilbert Murray, Jane Harrison, and George Thomson, did accumulate supporting evidence. But that began nearly half a century later. One of the reasons for the tumultuous reception of this book was this concerted refusal to support speculation with sufficient documentation. In view of Nietzsche's later career, we now see this as typical of him, aspiring to stimulate new research rather than carrying it out himself.

Nietzsche sees these primitive festivals as a "witches' brew" (*Hexentrank*) of sensuality and cruelty. This orgiastic picture of Dionysian rites recurs throughout antiquity, surviving even in Euripides' *Bacchae,* where intoxication with the god leads inexorably to murder. When this Dionysian religion comes to Greece, Nietzsche claims, a settlement is made that establishes boundary lines beteen Apollo and Dionysus, and even mutual respect. Here he may be alluding to the legalization of the cult inside Athens' city limits immediately after the coup of Peisistratos in 560 B.C. "At bottom, however, the chasm was not bridged over."

In ensuing passages Nietzsche elaborates what he means by the Dionysian, and it is really a double description:

1. First of all, the primordial "witches' brew" gives way to "the curious blending and duality in the emotions," that is, the physiological similarity of agony and ecstasy. One of Nietzsche's lifelong themes will be the necessity for embracing both joy and suffering gladly, in what he calls *amor fati* or "the love of destiny." Dionysus

emblematizes this ability to accept pleasure and pain as the opposite sides of the same coin. This theme recurs even in the last line of the book.

2. "Nature for the first time attains her artistic jubilee; . . . the destruction of the *principium individuationis* for the first time becomes an artistic phenomenon." Here the identification of Apollo with individuation appears strongly, along with its mirror image: the association of Dionysus with the individual's destruction and resultant reimmersion in the collective. What Nietzsche means by "nature" (*Natur*) here is simply the Dionysian—what a remarkable redefinition of the word! Nature is the species-awareness that comes from the utter destruction of individuation. In other words, it is something like Schopenhauer's Will.

Music establishes the boundaries between the Dionysian and the Apollinian. Apollo's music is architectonic, and rhythmic in the particular sense of poetic rhythm and meter. Dionysian music is above all melodic and harmonic, leading to the dance—"the entire symbolism of the body is called into play." This passage smacks of Schopenhauer and his identification of the body and the Will. Then yet another Schopenhauerian motif is introduced: the veil of Maya. Borrowed by Schopenhauer from Hinduism, *Maya* means "illusion." It refers to the fragility of the world of the senses. Look up from the book for a moment and imagine that whatever scene is before you is nothing more than a beautifully elaborate painting on cloth. Then imagine tearing the cloth. What would be behind it? Nietzsche claims that when the veil is torn, "nature" is revealed—that is, the Will, the true appetitive nature of the universe. At the tearing of this veil, individuated Apollo looks on in astonishment (*Erstaun*).

The closure of this section is crucial for what follows. Nietzsche presents the purported accommodation of Apollo and Dionysus as if it were historical. The Apollinian consciousness, when confronted with the interloper god Dionysus and his revelers, experiences the god first as foreign, and then as not so foreign. Greek consciousness, under the spell of Apollinian individuation and its delicate illusions (Maya), had forgotten the dark underlying oneness. This means that instead of fusing Apollo and Dionysus into some kind of synthetic middle ground, Nietzsche is making them *hierarchical*, establishing Dionysus as the formless source of the transitory formalism of Apollo. Dreams are concretions of the general intoxication, just as in Schopenhauer the Will is responsible even for our illusions—that veil of Maya.

Sections 3 and 4

Now Nietzsche proposes to deconstruct the "Apollinian culture" to reveal its foundations. He gives us an image of the edifice that is to be razed. High on its gables stand the gods, their deeds depicted in reliefs. Sketchy as this picture may be, it suggests the Parthenon, which had friezes of this kind along its principal horizontals. These figures were removed from Athens in 1812 through the efforts of the Earl of Elgin, a former British ambassador to Constantinople, who claimed (perhaps rightly) that they were in danger of destruction. In 1816 they were purchased by the British Museum, where they became known as the Elgin Marbles. They remain there today, despite widespread sentiment for returning them and interminable efforts by Greece to retrieve them.

Nietzsche did not see these figures in person, but they would have been well known to him through reproductions. They are a highly formal grouping, and their evocation here gives the Apollinian a more static feeling than one might think appropriate for gods and tragic heroes. This points up a tension that recurs throughout Nietzsche's discussion of the Apollinian. Sometimes he sees it as heroic, striving, struggling to maintain individuality in the face of the inevitable victory of anonymous nature. At other times, he seems to be drawn back into the traditional German idea of "Greek serenity," which comes from Winckelmann. Traces of this "contemplative Apollo" occur when Nietzsche is at his most mystical. In any case, the architecture of the

Parthenon is an appropriate figure for Nietzsche's hierarchical conception of the Apollinian rising out of the Dionysian earthworks.

First Nietzsche will tell us what these gods are *not*. He cautions us that we must not "approach these Olympians with another religion" in mind. "Another religion" is Nietzschean code for Christianity, against which he waged a lifelong ideological battle. His father, a Protestant minister who died when his son was only a young boy, left behind a family steeped in a narrow and rather unemotional Lutheran piety. It is possible to see Nietzsche's crusade against Christianity as a reaction to this upbringing, although throughout his career he remains an implacable enemy of *any* sort of prefabricated value system. Nietzsche believes that there is no such thing as final truth, that every statement presented as "true" must still be subjected to critical scrutiny. This is one of the things that make him a difficult philosopher: it is impossible to make a list of "things Nietzsche believes." Truths and conclusions matter less to him than the process by which values are (provisionally) established. And all systems of belief, because of their fixed and elaborate structures, preclude the free continuation of this process.

Much of this discussion of the Olympian pantheon may be seen as an oblique attack on Christian theology and ethics. To begin with, Nietzsche warns us not to expect any sort of moral example from the Olympians. They offer no ascetic, charitable, or even benevolent ideal—that is, no Christian virtue. These gods are, to use a phrase that would become one of Nietzsche's book titles, "beyond good and evil." Anyone who has studied Greek mythology even briefly knows that the Olympians do a great many things that the Christian Trinity does not. Greek gods change into animals and even material objects, often with the aim of copulating with mortals (although it can be argued that the Christian God does this once, in the form of a dove). Olympians do bloody battle with one another, steal things, commit treason, lie, bear grudges, play favorites, and wreak havoc on mortals. By Christian moral standards they are a bad lot.

More than that, however, they are distinguished from the Christian godhead by their utterly different attitude toward human life. The

A Reading

parable of Midas and Silenus serves mainly to pose the problem: does life's suffering outweigh all its positive qualities? The proposition that death or unbirth is preferable to life is a fairly standard formulation of Greek pessimism, and Nietzsche takes it as Dionysian wisdom, ultimately too dreadful for humans to face and still continue living, unless they construct some illusion to mitigate its hard truth. The Christian answer is to deny meaning to the world and its suffering by declaring the afterlife (i.e., death) to be a true, just, and eternal existence—everything this life is not. For this reason Christianity's principal visualization of God—Christ on the Cross—shows the divinity in his death-agony. This image points the believer in the desired direction—away from life on earth.

Nietzsche argues that the Olympians, on the contrary, were created to stand *between* the Greeks and the horror. They are depicted as living an idealized and immortal version of human life. This is why they are called "anthropomorphic" or "human-shaped" gods. They are life-affirming, in the face of insuperable odds, whereas the Christian divinity is life-denying even in its iconography.

Acknowledging the human condition to be immutable, the Olympians nonetheless offer consolation to mortals by means of their shining example of superior scope and freedom. Of course this "veiling" of the fate of humanity is just a deception, but Nietzsche implicitly finds it preferable to the denial of life. He describes Olympian joy evolving into beauty "just as roses burst from thorny bushes." The Olympian strategy for dealing with the horror confers beauty on the world, while the Christian strategy turns the world into a kind of hell, or at any rate a purgatory.

"Seducing one to a continuation of life"—this summarizes the function of the Olympians. Nietzsche calls them "bright sunshine," like the luminous sun of Greece. He cites the particular fear that Greeks felt at the prospect of dying and having to go down into the darkness of Hades. To merge with the luminous realm of the Olympians is analogous to living in "the *middle world* of art," where illusions (or "representations") can still be believed. From this point of view, it is no longer best not to be born; instead "to die soon is the worst of all for them, the next worst—to die at all." Life's value is (provisionally) reestablished in this way.

Art that accepts these illusions wholeheartedly is called "naive." This term requires some explanation. Running through this section are subtones of an essay by Johann Christoph Friedrich Schiller (1759–1805), the German romantic dramatist, historian, and critic. The essay, "Uber naive und sentimentalische Dichtung" ("On the Naive and Sentimental Poetry"), divides poets into the naive, who write out of a fundamental unity with nature, and the sentimental, who try to return to a lost ideal of nature. Naive poets write "naturally" and spontaneously, while the sentimental rely on formal and technical devices to attempt an unavoidably forced and nostalgic reunion with the natural world. This influential essay would certainly have been familiar to Nietzsche's readers, and he invokes it to clarify what he means by Apollinian art.

Like the Dionysian, which is its source, the Apollinian also comes from nature, from Dionysus. This is an important clarification, because it helps to illustrate Nietzsche's "anti-dialectic." Once again it would be easy, at this point in the essay, to see Apollo as "civilization" and Dionysus as the opposite—nature. Yet through the tragic age, civilization and nature were not opposed. This is almost a perfect echo of Schiller's definition of the naive. In all of their myriad aspects, Nietzsche sees the two gods always as extreme ends of a continuum, rather than as opposites. In this way he tries to get away from the formation of a simple, logical antinomy.

Homer is the foremost exemplar of the naive poet, since he himself fathers a literary tradition and therefore has no occasion to look backward and be "sentimental." This allows him to be part of the world he narrates, giving his work an immediacy, an archetypal, self-creating spontaneity. For Homer, nature and culture, war and poetry, are one and the same.

•   •   •

Likening the Apollinian Greek to a dreamer who does not want to awaken, Nietzsche then asserts the *superiority* of dreams to waking life (an echo of Schopenhauer's "leaves of one and the same book") and expresses a longing "for redemption through illusion." In so doing, he himself takes on the role of the sentimental artist.

Art created out of belief in illusion would be a kind of metaillusion, or as Nietzsche puts it, sounding like Schopenhauer again, "mere appearance of mere appearance." At one point he speaks of this as a "demotion," but he plainly has a "sentimental" admiration for it. Since (like actual dreams) this dream art can take place only in individual consciousness ("quietly in his tossing bark, amid the waves"), it is necessary to take account of the way the individualism of this art shapes it. The boundaries of individual consciousness exert a formal limitation and generate two laws of limitation that apply to such art: "know thyself" and "nothing in excess."

"Know thyself" (*gnothi seauton*) is the commonest proverb of all Greek antiquity, occurring from the beginning of recorded time to the late days of the Hellenistic decadence. It eventually became a kind of cliché, but its original meaning was an important one for the Greeks. It is a little like the Confucian formulation that Ezra Pound translated as: "If a man have not order within him / He can not spread order about him."[7] Ignoring this wisdom creates "overweening pride," or *hubris,* one of the commonest "tragic flaws." A lack of self-knowledge, to the Greek mind, makes all other knowledge impossible. This is particularly obvious in reference to a dreamlike art form.

"Nothing in excess" (*meden agan*) is perhaps second only to "know thyself" in frequency of occurrence among Greek proverbs. It is thought to be Pythagorean in origin, having reference to the geometrical model upon which that philosopher based his ethics, cosmology, aesthetics, and musicology. It refers to internal proportions. An excessively long side to a rectangle used in the design of a building or the frame of a painting will destroy the beauty of that creation. A rhythmical, harmonic, or melodic excess can destroy the appeal of a piece of music. So too, any behavioral excess can ruin the harmonious proportions of a person's character. Highly internalized Apollinian art must obey this law as well, and this accounts for its formal sophistication.

Apollinian art, then, reflects a fully individuated self, satisfactory both in its self-awareness and in its formal proportions. To add some life to this theorizing, Nietzsche goes on to try to situate Apollinian art in history, placing it between the age of the Titans and the coming of Dionysus. The Titans, a race of gods that preceded the Olympians and were overthrown by them, were earlier described by Nietzsche as ruling by terror, and they are indeed a far less endearing pantheon than the Olympian one. The Apollinian dreamworld attempts to transcend suffering by luminous dreams, whereas the Titans do not seek to alleviate suffering at all, but rather use it as a tool to retain power.

Now for the coming of Dionysus. Rejected at first as a barbarian god, Dionysus serves to remind Apollinians that their dreamworld was originally a response to suffering. Dionysus in effect brings with him a memory of the Titanic age and its overt terror. For Dionysus, as we will see, does not share the Apollinian strategy of veiling the horror and suffering of life with dreamlike illusions. Dionysus *relishes* the suffering, because it is so integral a part of life. "Apollo could not live without Dionysus!" because recognizing life's horror and suffering creates the need for illusion. And so the relationship of these two gods, the embodiments of two modes of being, is certainly not dialectical opposition after all. It is more like symbiosis, or mutual dependency.

Nietzsche illustrates this with a remarkable bit of imagery: the noise of the Dionysian festival intruding upon the contemplative sound of the Apollinian harp. It is typical of Nietzsche's literary style that he will suddenly incarnate some of his most disembodied speculations in spare, vivid poetic images. We have already noted one of these—the vision of the Apollinian in the storm-tossed boat. As if in response to the "demonic folk-song" he hears as Dionysian music, his prose builds up to the cry of Silenus, "Woe! woe!" The studied, serene art of Apollo is challenged, and reminded of its origins.

"*Excess* revealed itself as truth." Dionysian art attacks the Apollinian principle of *meden agan,* "nothing in excess." In the same way it attacks the principle, "know thyself." What Dionysian art demands is "forget thyself." For the art of intoxication dissolves the individual into the body of collective consciousness, where the self no longer has any meaning. And this state of intoxication cannot be attained by moderation, by avoiding excess. Quite the contrary.

Sparta is introduced as evidence that Apollinian consciousness reacted to the advent of Dionysus by becoming rigid, by creating a dictatorial political power to defend its precious illusions. The calm man in the boat, weathering the stormy sea, is now chained to the oarlocks just in case.

We then come to a new period in Greek art. To review for a moment, Nietzsche has taken us from the Titanic period, time of terror; to the Apollinian age that began with the epics of Homer; to the coming of Dionysus, when the Apollinian "hardening" into the Doric (Spartan) began. And now comes the age when Dionysus and Apollo discover "their common goal."

Nietzsche is finally getting to the subject of tragedy.

Section 5

In the opening paragraph of section 1, Nietzsche compared the Apollinian and the Dionysian to the two sexes. What he does in the ensuing sections is to suggest a history of these two modes, while explaining the essence of each of them. At the start of section 5 he brings us back to the point of union between these "sexes," whose offspring will be tragic art.

This sexual imagery may seem a little corny in the late 1980s, but it must be remembered that Nietzsche was writing within the confines of a puritanical Protestant bourgeois society, so that such metaphors and locutions were more provocative to his contemporaries than they are to us. What seems suggestive in them is meant to lend a subliminal force to the reader's impression of Dionysus. Puritanical societies usually fear overt emotions, particularly love, and they dread any form of disorder and mass activity. Dionysus, then, suggests everything Nietzsche's readers might well fear the most.

At this point it should be clear that although Nietzsche is

ostensibly writing about Greek antiquity, on another level he is creating a moral allegory about the modern world in general, and his own country in particular. He is suggesting that the remedy for the malaise of the late nineteenth century, its *mal du siècle* or "century sickness," is a renewed acquaintance with the Dionysian powers of collective intoxication. The specter of drunken and riotous mobs rolling through the streets of Leipzig in the 1870s would have elicited an anxiety comparable to those created by today's principal bugbears: overpopulation, terrorism, nuclear annihilation, and so on.

At this point Nietzsche tips his hand and attacks his own era's preference for "objective" or disinterestedly contemplative art. He introduces the figure of Archilochus as a foil for Homer. "Compared with Homer, Archilochus appalls us by his cries of hatred and scorn, by his drunken outbursts of desire." Why Archilochus? First, he is one of the few known literary figures who may possibly date as far back as Homer. Second, Archilochus was an earthy poet who had a reputation in antiquity for writing particularly vicious poems against his enemies, though none of these works has survived. He earned his living not by the harp and the recitation of epic poems, but as a mercenary soldier (an occupation held in particular contempt by the military ethics of ancient Greece). Many of his extant works are full of the cynicism of a soldier of fortune. War instilled in him a sense of the transience and unimportance of any individual life. So scandalous was Archilochus's work that the iamb, a metric foot he used frequently, was held in disgrace for the rest of classical antiquity. To be able to discredit an entire poetic rhythm—now that's genuine infamy! Worse yet, there is a poem of Archilochus in which he dares to praise something more intolerable than hate and evil—mediocrity.

Nietzsche extrapolates from this contrasting of Homer and Archilochus to make a new contrast between Apollinian and Dionysian art. This time it is a difference of literary genre. Apollo is associated with "objective" epic poetry, and Dionysus with the "subjective" lyric. Eventually Nietzsche will reject the categories of objective and subjective, but he employs them for the time being throughout this section. This leads to a rather confusing contradiction with some of what he has said before.

A Reading

Apollinian art has heretofore been characterized as individualistic, an expression of the *principium individuationis*, the solitary figure in the storm-tossed boat, while Dionysian art has been characterized by the submersion of the individual ego in orgiastic collective song. The difficulty here begins with the term *lyrist*, which seems to suggest Apollo's lyre as opposed to Dionysus's flute. It also suggests the modern word *lyricist*, which denotes the author of a song's words ("lyrics") as opposed to its music. In fact, by "lyrist" Nietzsche means *the author of lyric poems*, that is, of nonepic, nonnarrative poems—Archilochus rather than Homer.

Unfortunately the problems are only beginning at this point; straightening out the terminology is not enough to clear the air. For despite the supposed "individuation" of Apollinian art, epic poets rarely use "I," the first person singular pronoun, except (as in the *Odyssey*) in the opening invocation of the Muse, or in reporting dialogue, when the "I" is someone other than the poet speaking. Lyric poets, on the other hand, use the "I" for the direct expression of the poet's "subjectivity." This seems to run counter to Nietzsche's assertion that lyric art is Dionysian, and therefore collective in nature. What's going on here?

Two preliminary points apply. First, because of his unorthodox method, Nietzsche is not afraid of contradicting himself. Despite his denial of dialectic logic, the philosophical tradition in which he was educated left him with the notion that contradiction leads not necessarily to absurdity but to greater scope. Second, throughout the entire *Birth of Tragedy* whenever Nietzsche is arguing one-on-one with Schopenhauer, he becomes rather confusing. What we are seeing here is a young philosopher trying to establish his own identity apart from that of his main influence. All artists and thinkers go through a similar process of "intellectual puberty" in their early works. Much of the "Attempt at Self-Criticism" in the 1886 introduction hinges on these confrontations with Schopenhauer, which often lead to the most obscure passages in the work. What follows here is thus necessarily an artificial and not entirely successful attempt to justify the contradictions in this section—bearing in mind that such contradictions are not meant to be neatly resolved.

If Dionysian lyric poets further the destruction of the *principium individuationis*, why is it that such poets use the "I" so much? The crucial sentence here is this one: "When Archilochus, the first Greek lyrist, proclaims to the daughters of Lycambes both his mad love and his contempt, it is not his passion alone that dances before us in orgiastic frenzy; but we see Dionysus and the Maenads, we see the drunken reveler Archilochus sunk down in slumber." In other words, the apparently subjective lyric poet uses the "I" to express *universal* passions, emotions that are not narrowly his own. This kind of poet thus seeks a path *through* the individual ego to the collective. He becomes typical. "The artist has already surrendered his subjectivity in the Dionysian process." Nietzsche sees both kinds of art not as fixed *products* alone, but as *processes*.

Conversely, the epic poet generates images, not the "musical mood" that Nietzsche, quoting Schiller, ascribes to the Dionysian. The Apollinian plastic or epic artist "never grows tired of contemplating lovingly even [these images'] minutest traits." It doesn't even matter whether the images in question are of passion and emotion; the Apollinian act of contemplation interiorizes them within the individual. "Thus, by this mirror of illusion, [the Apollinian artist] is protected against becoming one and fused with his figures." In other words, the Dionysian moves from the individual to the collective, whereas the Apollinian goes in the opposite direction.

There is a terminological component to this discussion as well. As we said earlier, Nietzsche is trying to transcend what he regards as a useless distinction between "subjective" and "objective" art. It is to this end that he presents his long quotation from Schopenhauer, which leads to the notion that "the whole opposition between the subjective and the objective, which Schopenhauer still uses as a measure of value in classifying the arts, is altogether irrelevant in aesthetics." The gist of the following rather obscure sentences is this: that the opposition of subjectivity and objectivity is a false one, since subject implies object and object implies subject. Each term is meaningless without the other. Nietzsche closes the section with an invocation of "genius," which understands the ultimate unity of subject and object.

A Reading

There is a similar argument against the subject-object opposition in Samuel Taylor Coleridge's *Biographia Literaria*. "Subject" refers to a conscious, perceiving being; "object" to the thing perceived, whether that thing is a material object or a conscious entity. In other words, if you look at me, I am the object of your perception even though I myself am conscious. The old philosophical debate over whether a tree falling in the forest would make a sound is based on the notion that nothing can be an object of perception if there is no subject present. Coleridge suggests that the entire subject-object distinction is worthless because each term is meaningful only in terms of the other. A subject with nothing to perceive would not be a subject, because it would not be perceiving. Likewise, an object without a subject would not be an object at all, because it is not perceived. There is something self-creating about the distinction. Perhaps it is nothing more than a terminological sleight of hand. Or else we must understand that when we speak of subjectivity and objectivity we are speaking of a *relationship* rather than an opposition. Nietzsche, like Coleridge, wants to establish that relationship without the idea of logical opposition. Thus Homer and Archilochus, and Apollo and Dionysus, are in some sense necessary complements of each other.

This closing passage, for all its difficulty, is one of the most famous in the book. Having dismissed the distinction between subject and object, Nietzsche goes on to argue that there is a "primordial artist of the world" with which the genius must merge, must "coalesce." This is Nietzsche's version of Hegel's *An-Sich-Für-Sich*, or total unity of subject and object. This primordial artist of the world does not exist for our education or betterment, but only to assert the aesthetic universe. That is the meaning of this famous phrase, so often quoted out of context: "It is only as an *aesthetic phenomenon* that existence and the world are eternally *justified*." And this justification is possible only when genius can overcome the trivializing distinction between "objective" and "subjective" forms of art.

Nietzsche continues to prepare for his presentation of tragedy as the highest example of such an art.

Sections 6, 7, and 8

In these sections, Nietzsche comes to a crucial part of his argument: the origin and nature of the tragic chorus. First, however, he discusses the folk song, ascribing its origins to Archilochus, the prototypical Dionysian poet.

Folk songs do not remain a purely Dionysian art; the process of adding words presents a kind of preliminary instance of the union of Apollo and Dionysus. The song's words are seen as an Apollinian manifestation. But the melodic or Dionysian aspect of the folk song is seen as the "substratum and prerequisite." "*Melody is therefore primary and universal.*"

The stanzaic structure of folk songs shows that "language is strained to its utmost that it may *imitate music*"; this is contrasted with the "steady flow" of epic narration. In section 5, Schiller is quoted as ascribing primacy to the "musical mood" in the act of poetic composition; here the same point is made for the folk song. The way words are added to songs is analogous to the way instrumental music conjures up images in our minds, which Nietzsche sees as language imitating music. Music doesn't need words, "but merely *endures* them as accompaniments."

To emphasize this point, Nietzsche returns to the terminology of Schopenhauer. Music, although it is not Will in itself, is a manifestation of Will, of primordial desire, while words are like phenomena or "representations." The "lyrist" in folk songs generates words through the Apollinian imaging process, all the while aware that music has its own energy and impetus. Nietzsche is echoing the image of the calm Apollinian in the boat on a tempestuous sea. The sea is music, and the words are, in effect, the boat.

This is rather close to Richard Wagner's theorizing about opera, where the orchestra is envisioned as a kind of ocean of Schopenhauerian Will, with the singers floating upon that turbulent water. Wagner felt that the orchestra should never stop and start again, as it does in traditional Italian-style opera, which is divided into "numbers." In

A Reading

Wagner's mature operas the orchestra keeps flowing without a stop. Instead of discrete arias, the sung portions flow out of and back into the orchestra, as if the stage characters were merely momentary individuations destined to be subsumed back into the collective and anonymous instrumental music. Echoes of this Wagnerian application of Schopenhauer are strong in this passage. The aim is to prove that music in the folk song is primary, and the words secondary.

Now Nietzsche makes the same argument for tragedy that he just made for the folk song, trying to establish music as primary and dialogue as secondary. The musical component of tragedy is the chorus. Although in many modern performances of Greek tragedies the chorus gives only a collective recitation, there is no doubt that in Greek antiquity music and dance were the heart of their performance. Here we run across a unique and rather depressing historical fact: of all the universe of ancient Greek music, we do not possess so much as a single note. To be sure, fragmentary examples of musical notation do survive, but how to translate them into actual sound is an almost hopeless proposition. It is therefore easy for theorists of tragedy to forget the musical basis of the chorus, since only the words survive. For this reason, theorists before Nietzsche spend a good deal of time trying to decide just what purpose the chorus is supposed to serve, what it is doing there at all.

Choruses rarely advance the progress of the plot in Greek tragedy. Like one of their modern equivalents, Shakespearean soliloquies, they are frequently *reactions* rather than actions. They are interpolated lyric poems sung by a group of nameless characters—who constitute, in effect, a kind of *collective character*. In the earliest extant tragedies, the chorus takes up a large share of the plays' stage time, while in later tragedies, such as those of Euripides, it is often reduced to the role of a musical interlude. Most of the major theoreticians of tragedy from Aristotle to Hegel therefore consign the chorus to a secondary position in both the structure and the evolution of tragedy. Hegel and Schopenhauer ignore the chorus almost completely, concentrating on the named characters and the plots in which they participate. Nietzsche will suggest something entirely new—that the chorus, tragedy's

Dionysian unit, actually existed before the named characters and ought to be regarded as the basis of the art.

Nietzsche now sets about refuting some of the previous theories of the role of the chorus. First, he attacks the notion that the chorus is meant to be a theatrical representation of "the people," who somehow outlive the excesses of their kings. In the wake of the great liberal revolutions in America and France, many nineteenth-century theorists sought to find models for modern democracies in the city-states of ancient Greece, particularly Athens. In fact, democracy was only an intermittent condition in most Greek city-states. Most of the time a king or "tyrant" (from the Greek word *turannos,* which doesn't have the nasty connotations of its modern descendant) would move in to assume power after a period of unstable democracy. Some tyrants, like Peisistratos, whose reign led to the legalization of the Dionysian religion and eventually to the birth of tragedy, may have brought democratic reforms with them as part of the political package. But democracy, then as now, is a fragile form of social organization.

Those who see antique Greece as the "birthplace of democracy" (to use a cliché common in American high schools) tend to see tragic choruses as representatives of the common people, watching kings, heroes, and tyrants make a mess of things. Nietzsche argues against this by saying that tragedy exists from the start in a religious realm, and not in a sociopolitical one. He claims that "the whole opposition of prince and people" was simply not present at that point in history. You will notice, however, that he doesn't really prove this point. Here Nietzsche is tacitly following his own antidemocratic tendencies. In much of his later work he argues at great length that the mass of people are meant to be slaves and that a democratic regime would be nothing more than a reduction of civilization to mere herd behavior. He spares us this line of reasoning at the present time, though, and moves on to refute another common hypothesis about the chorus: that it is a representative of the audience, a kind of "ideal spectator."

The theorist he chooses to take on is one A. W. Schlegel (1767–1845), brother of the famous romantic critic Friedrich Schlegel and a great translator of Shakespeare into German. Most of Schlegel's remarks on tragedy are to be found in a volume entitled *Lectures on*

A Reading

Dramatic Art and Literature (1809–11). Nietzsche's dismissal of this thesis, like his rejection of the "democratic" theory of the chorus, is based upon his contempt for the mass of ordinary people. He thinks so little of the average spectator that he cannot conceive of an "ideal" one. Besides, he goes on, the audience always remains aware that it is seeing a play, whereas the chorus "really" believes in the existence of the tragic protagonists. Nietzsche sarcastically wonders whether it is "characteristic of the ideal spectator to run onto the stage and free the god from his torments." In other words, Nietzsche finds it useless or worse to confuse the audience with the characters on stage. This confusion could lead to the idea that a tragic performance was all performers and no spectators. "The spectator without the spectacle is an absurd notion" (rather like the subject without an object).

Schiller is once again invoked in his claim that the chorus ensures that nothing on stage will be taken as real, that the chorus is the beginning of a war "against all naturalism in art." Nietzsche approves of this as a starting point, at any rate. Tragedy—Aristotle and his mimesis notwithstanding—does not mirror the real world. Nietzsche sees the original chorus as a group of satyrs, mythic creatures half-man and half-goat, sacred to Dionysus. The word *tragedy* apparently comes from the Greek word *tragus*, goat. *Tragedy* seems to mean something like "goat-song." This etymology would support Nietzsche's idea of a prototypic satyr chorus, reminding "civilized" people of their tribal origins and their proximity to the animal kingdom. There is no confusing the realm of satyrs with the realm of ordinary life; this is all too obvious. "The chasm of oblivion separates the worlds of everyday reality and of the Dionysian reality."

Hamlet is introduced as analogous to Dionysian man. Hamlet thinks too much to act; his realization is that temporal action cannot effect eternal change in the world. To believe that action could be useful requires illusions—and this is where the Apollinian stage characters appear. Their illusions about value in the world allow them to act, to advance the plot of the play. The Dionysian *gnosis* (privileged or esoteric knowledge) sees too deeply into the horror of existence to subscribe to such illusions. And yet it provokes their birth.

The satyr is not to be confused with its modern shadow, the

shepherd-figure common to pastoral poetry. The shepherd reflects a longing to return to the simplicity of nature—he is a "sentimental" figure, where the satyr is "naive," that is, primordial. The satyr embodies Dionysian revelry and sexual intoxication, and cuts to the core of "reality" and "civilization," exposing them as lies. Once again Nietzsche identifies the Dionysian with the "thing-in-itself" and the civilized world with mere appearances, what he earlier calls the "veil of Maya." Even when the chorus eventually comes to take human rather than satyr form, its fidelity to this goatlike prototype of the Dionysian reveler remains.

Throughout this passage, Nietzsche alludes to the architectural form of the Greek theater, and this is one of the most impressive bits of evidence for his theory. The performance space in the City Dionysia does indeed resemble "a lonely valley in the mountains." The audience is seated in rows rising upward and away from the ground-level stage. An altar to Dionysus, vestige of the original religious purpose of the theater, stands in the center. A flight of steps leading to a pair of large doors rises to the rear, but otherwise the Dionysia is nearly a theater-in-the-round. The area surrounding the altar is a dance floor for the chorus, while the actors portraying named characters often declaim from the steps and enter and exit through the doors. In other words, the very design of the Greek theater seems to uphold both Nietzsche's view of its religious origins and the literal, physical centrality of the choric component of the plays.

Now to the point: the dithyramb or hymn to Dionysus is different from all other forms of song in that its singer loses track of himself as an individual and moves into the timeless and collective world of the god's servants. The chorus that performs this ego-effacing song in turn generates new individuations: the stage characters of tragedy. This is Nietzsche's greatest contribution to the theory of tragedy: the notion that the stage figures are not merely imported from Homeric epic and Olympian mythology, and then given a musical accompaniment; the notion that music came first, and that actors rose from the music to take on provisional individual identities. The emotional power of tragedy comes not from the poignancies of its plotting, but from the combination of suffering and ecstasy that Dionysus imbues in his followers. Dionysus is therefore the hidden hero of every tragic drama. The stage actors in Greek tragedy performed in masks. But what is under the mask? Is it a human face? Or the face of Dionysus?

This explains the difference between the language of the chorus and that of the stage figures. The chorus delivers song lyrics, with musical and terpsichorean movements: strophe (turn), antistrophe (counterturn), and epode (stasis or stand). The stage figures use "the clarity and firmness of epic." The Apollinians move in linear progressions through the events of the plot, whereas the chorus moves cyclically through its dance, recapitulating the cycle of the seasons that is sacred to Dionysus, the agrarian god.

Section 9

The Apollinian is now redefined by its relationship to the Dionysian. Nietzsche inaugurates this section with a metaphor: Just as we see dark spots in our vision after staring at the sun, so after staring into total darkness we see flecks of light. This is how he introduces tragedy's Apollinian heroes and how he describes their relationship to the Dionysian chorus.

The serenity and grandeur of tragic heroes and their language can easily be mistaken for a cheerful obliviousness to danger and terror, just as the chorus can be mistaken for a mere musical interlude. But Nietzsche's argument for the primacy of the chorus puts the heroes before us in an altogether new perspective. We now see them as *issuing from* the chorus, diamonds forged from the intensity of collective choric energy. This makes the stage characters dependent on the chorus for their very existence.

Nietzsche turns to Oedipus, hero of Sophocles' *Oedipus the King* and *Oedipus at Colonus*. Although these two plays are not in fact from the same trilogy (all Greek tragedies were performed in groups of three called trilogies, followed by a slapstick satyr play), Nietzsche treats them as if there were nonetheless a continuity between them. In the first play, Oedipus's quest for the cause of an epidemic in his city of Thebes leads to the revelation that he himself is at fault, having unknowingly murdered his father and married his mother. This angers the gods, who then punish the whole city for their tyrant's impurity. He who appears to be a civilized and responsible king, fulfilling his duty to his people by investigating the plague, is recast as a criminal against nature; he puts out his eyes in contrition for his "blindness" about his past and goes voluntarily into exile. *Oedipus at Colonus* shows the king at the end of that exile, transfigured by the gods even as he goes to his death.

In these two plays, Nietzsche finds the essence of the Apollinian dilemma. By examining the fabric of reality too closely, Oedipus rediscovers its horror and relearns the "abominable" Dionysian wisdom. Famous for solving the riddle of the Sphinx, Oedipus is ultimately condemned to solve his own. Nietzsche argues that the suffering of Oedipus is the suffering of all those who seek the truth of nature. And yet at the end of that suffering comes a delicate and ineffable redemption—the bright spot after darkness (or after blindness). The path to this redemption, according to Nietzsche, consists in *giving up* one's active (Apollinian) nature and *giving in* to the passive aspect of Dionysian consciousness. This is, once again, a Schopenhauerian idea, a recognition of the illusory nature of the phenomenal world. Returned to the more primitive state of Will, against which individual volition is powerless, Oedipus accedes to a kind of wisdom. It is a wisdom that denies the dreamlike constructions of kingship, duty, civilization in general—but that affirms a transcendental joy that comes from suffering and the dissolution of the individual. It is, to invoke another Greek truism, *pathei mathos*, or "wisdom through suffering."

Turning to Aeschylus's *Prometheus*, Nietzsche speaks of the "glory of activity" (the Apollinian) and the "glory of passivity" (the Dionysian). All the active world, gods and heroes alike, exists in mutual dependency: the Olympian gods are created by humanity's desire for illusion, therefore these gods need humanity for their very existence. But humanity needs the gods as objectifications of their "civilized" illusions. Prometheus, who created the human race, emblematizes this. As one of the primordial Titans, he is unavoidably at odds with the Olympians who overthrew his pantheon. His creations, the humans, provide him with a new matrix of values once the Titans are destroyed; for humanity he is willing to endure torture at the hands of Zeus, including incarceration in the sealed vault of Tartarus, deep in the core of the earth.

Because Prometheus, and not Zeus, is the creator of the human race, Greek mythology suggests humanity's association with forces earlier and more elemental than the Olympians, powers less illusory and Apollinian. Using racial (and perhaps racist) terminology borrowed from Wagner, Nietzsche suggests that the myth of Prometheus possesses for the Aryans a significance similar to that of the Fall for the Semites. To be sure, Prometheus as Aeschylus depicts him is a fallen god, as Adam is a fallen man. But there is more to Nietzsche's comparison than that analogue alone. There is something like original sin in the way Prometheus gave fire to humans, without asking for the kind of human-god reciprocity that, as we have just seen, is central to the nature of the Olympian pantheon. Through the emblem of fire, it becomes clear that suffering is the price that must be paid for human autonomy. This is the same message conveyed by the Old Testament emblem of the apple, fruit of the Tree of Knowledge. But Nietzsche argues that Semitic "original sin" is not tragic because it results from weakness alone, whereas in Prometheus there is a more genuinely tragic impulse, the *active* embrace of the human condition—that is, trading happiness for autonomy.

At this point, Nietzsche verges closer to Hegel's theory of tragedy than he does anywhere else in the essay. Hegel's general metaphysical views are discussed in the first chapter of this commentary, but now it is necessary to take a brief look at the theory of tragedy incorporated in his *Aesthetics* in order to understand how it is affecting Nietzsche at this point in *The Birth of Tragedy.*

Hegel, you will recall, hypothesizes an Absolute Spirit that contains the sum of all human consciousness. This spirit is in a perpetual state of Becoming, striving to reach complete self-awareness by working through logical contraries—thesis and antithesis—toward syntheses that in turn become new theses. So what is the role of the individual in the progress of this superhuman mind? The basic assumption is that, by the collective nature of the Absolute, every individual contributes to the Absolute's progress merely by being conscious. There are, however, certain individuals who attain an especial status with reference to the Absolute. Most of this is contained in Hegel's theory of history, which he sees, not surprisingly, as cyclic, as an enactment of thesis, antithesis, and synthesis. Chronometric time is thus defined on the model of "logical time." In the progress of history, certain individuals come to embody some "substance" of the Absolute itself, come to stand for more than themselves alone. These are the World-Historical Individuals; they are at once supremely themselves, and at the same time they are more than mere individuals. They come to incarnate whole motions of history itself.

They are, put another way, examples of the perfect unity of subject and object. They are not describable merely in terms of the "objective" universal laws of existence, nor of the "subjective" laws of individual consciousness. When they act, their actions carry with them all the force of the Absolute itself and its rational movement toward self-realization. Without going into detail, suffice it to say that for Hegel tragic heroes cannot be mere individuals, but must possess in one way or another some of the "substance" of the Absolute.

Hegel saw as the highest form of tragic conflict and heroism one in which the tragic hero (or heroes) gains the status of World-Historical Individual by embodying some of "the *ethical* substance of the Absolute." Tragic conflict *cannot* be fought between someone possessing this substance and someone not so graced. Tragedy at its purest is the conflict of right and right, not right and wrong, and not, certainly, wrong and wrong. Hegel's favorite tragedy is Sophocles' *Antigone*, where two protagonists, King Creon and Antigone herself, come into conflict over the burying of the body of Polyneices, who is Creon's son and Antigone's brother. A traitor to Thebes, Polyneices was slain as he led an insurgent army against his father's regime. Creon, obeying the ethical imperative of the State, orders that the body be left unburied—a dreadful fate in the Greek scheme of life-after-death, where the spirit of an unburied body can never cross Lethe and attain forgetfulness. Antigone, obeying the ethical imperative of the Family, asserts that no one should leave the body and soul of a family member to such a fate. Who is right?

Believing that both political and familial imperatives contain some measure of "ethical substance," Hegel argues that both are right and that Sophocles' play is therefore the clearest illustration of tragic action. Antigone buries her brother's body. And then Creon seals her up in a tomb as punishment. When he ceases to act as a World-Historical Individual, Creon, too late, goes to the tomb and finds his daughter dead as well, bringing about the dissolution of his ruling house. Both sides are right; but both are equally and symmetrically defeated—just as both thesis and antithesis are in effect destroyed every time synthesis is reached. All tragic denouement is thus for Hegel a dissolution of the conflict, but without victory for either side. Instead, a whole new world order in which the conflict has been somehow transcended (synthesized) is put into place, and the Absolute marches on toward perfection.

The trouble with this theory is that it places all its emphasis upon the plot and the actions performed by the stage characters. It takes no account whatever of the chorus and certainly does not allocate it any structural importance in the plays. Hegel's is thus the most Apollinian of theories. It is at this point in *The Birth of Tragedy*, when Nietzsche is discussing the nature of the Apollinian, that he comes nearest to invoking Hegel:

> The contradiction at the heart of the world reveals itself . . . as a clash of worlds, e.g. of a divine and human one, in which each, taken as an individual, has right on its side, but nevertheless has to suffer for its individuation. . . . In the heroic attempt of the individual to attain universality, in the attempt to transcend the curse of

individuation and to become the *one* world-being, he suffers in his own person the primordial contradiction that is concealed in things, which means that he commits sacrilege and suffers.

Another problem with Hegel's theory is that, at least in his treatment of classical tragedy, he makes his point most clearly in his discussion of *Antigone,* with that play's unusual dual protagonists. Nietzsche, even while echoing Hegel, clarifies this "contradiction" (as he calls it in the quotation above) by containing it within a single hero. What Nietzsche is saying, in effect, is that Hegel's influential theory does indeed apply—but only to the actions of stage figures, only to the Apollinians. As such, it can tell only half the story, and perhaps not the really important half.

In this section Nietzsche is in effect proposing first Oedipus and then Prometheus as his own perfect tragic heroes, his answer to Hegel's Antigone. Oedipus and Prometheus each illustrate an important aspect of tragic heroism. Oedipus exemplifies the tragic "fall" from Apollinian individuation into Dionysian, collective existence. And Prometheus, no Olympian but a Titan fusing Apollinian and Dionysian elements, demonstrates the tragic mating of the two gods. In addition, Prometheus stands for humanity, in that humanity, too, is an admixture of these two gods and their modes of being. From this it can be inferred that human existence is in some respect tragic and that tragic drama is the perfect reflection of the human condition. This is the message contained in the introduction of another Titan, Atlas, who carries the world (i.e., the whole burden of earthly existence) on his shoulders. The supporting role of Atlas and the creational role of Prometheus give them status something like that of Hegel's World-Historical Individuals—that is, they retain strong individuation while dedicating themselves to the fundaments (Will, collectivity, intoxication) of existence that are otherwise said, in the *Birth of Tragedy,* to be Dionysian.

Nietzsche closes this section with more water imagery, comparing the individual to the wave and the Dionysian collectivity to the lake as a whole. This metaphor is reminiscent once again of Richard Wagner and his concept of singers floating upon the sea of the orchestra. The waves are Apollinian because they are *formal*. The Dionysian is a tide, perpetrator of formless energy. Tragedy recognizes both of these impulses and brings them into harmony. "All that exists is just and unjust and equally justified in both." The presentation of a contradiction in this way, followed by an assertion that both its poles are right, concludes this most Hegelian of passages. Regardless of philosophical precedents, this section is a crucial one for the development of the "anti-dialectic" that is at the heart of the book. It is also an important cadence in the argument, leading up to (one would think) a thorough account of the announced subject: the birth of tragedy.

Sections 10 and 11

Section 10 contains one of the great peculiarities of *The Birth of Tragedy*. About one-third of the way through his text, Nietzsche has at last established his components of tragedy, and at the start of this section he appears ready to give what his title promises: a complete account of how tragic drama came to be. As soon as the subject is at hand, however, he skips directly to what may be the *real* subject of his book: the *death* of tragedy.

Despite the section's opening sentence, the claim that "Greek tragedy in its earliest form had for its sole theme the sufferings of Dionysus" is anything but undisputed. Not only is a claim this bald not to be found in previous theoretical literature, it has hardly received universal support *since* Nietzsche. The proposition that all tragic heroes are masks of Dionysus is crucial here, for the Greek practice of masking actors is a strong metaphor for the provisional nature of their individuality. The heroic individual is an illusion, to be reabsorbed into Dionysian tribal anonymity the moment the heroic mask is removed.

This masking is the work of the illusion-weaving god Apollo, but what is masked is always Dionysus. Individuation is likened to the autumn ritual of Dionysus, in which the whole god is torn into (individual) pieces; accordingly it is perceived as pain. The hero's fall expresses the impulse to put the fragments of Dionysus back together. This may account for the curiously mixed feelings that a viewer has at the end of a tragedy. While it is dreadful to see a beautifully masked Apollinian suffer and fall, there is, at the same instant, a reassertion of a collective wisdom that Nietzsche links with the coming of spring and the rebirth of Dionysus.

These characters out of Homeric epic are now transfigured by their service to another god. They are not merely undigested bits of epic tradition taken out of context and sent onstage with a little musical accompaniment; rather, they are utterly changed. They are no longer figments of Apollinian dream-making; now they are poignantly transitory fragments returning to the original unity.

Once again, we are reminded that it is music that accomplished this historical regeneration of myth. The Olympian religion was atrophying, deteriorating into "juvenile history." That is, myths born of supernature and magic were distilled into systems that organized them to death. "[T]he feeling for myth perishes, and its place is taken by the claim of religion to historical foundations." This is the fate of all religions, perhaps. But the advent of Dionysus revitalized Greek myth, just when it was becoming "official" and losing its numinous content.

Now begins the long scrutiny of tragedy's death. The first scapegoat for its decline from the heights of Aeschylus and Sophocles (both of whom Nietzsche has already extolled at least briefly) is Euripides, who allegedly abandoned music as the wellspring of tragedy and attempted to supplant a drama of gods and heroes with a drama of ordinary human beings. This observation, with a different value judgment, is not unique to Nietzsche. From the practitioners of New Comedy, whom Nietzsche hates so roundly, to critics of the present day, Euripides is often *praised* for "humanizing" the highly conventionalized theater of Athens. Not that Euripides' characters aren't also drawn from the Homeric epics and the Olympian pantheon; they are.

A Reading

Most of the time, the case for Euripides' realism is made in terms of his language, which is less rhetorical and metrically rigid than that of Aeschylus and Sophocles. Ordinary concerns come to the surface, bringing with them an immediacy of characterization that is less forbidding than the grandeur and awe inspired by an Aeschylean or Sophoclean protagonist. Why is Nietzsche so set against Euripides' innovations, which are credited by many with revitalizing the theater and prolonging the life of tragic art?

First of all, Nietzsche's view of the origin and importance of the chorus would tend to bias him against Euripides, who did indeed diminish the importance of the choruses, making them more like musical interludes than collective foundations for tragic action. Furthermore, you will remember Nietzsche's arguments against the theory of the chorus as "ideal spectator," where he wonders what sense it would make to have spectators of any sort on stage. Now he accuses Euripides of pandering to the audience's desire to see its own image reflected in art. "Through [Euripides] the everyday man forced his way from the spectators' seats onto the stage. . . . Civic mediocrity, on which Euripides built all his political hopes, was now given a voice, while heretofore the demigod in tragedy . . . had determined the character of the language." To be sure, part of this opposition to Euripides is based upon Nietzsche's own dislike of democracy, an ideology that would give power to "the herd," making all excellence and nobility impossible.

"Why should the artist be bound to accommodate himself to a power whose strength lies solely in numbers?" For numbers, to Nietzsche, constitute democracy's only claim to power. He hates the leveling effect that such a redistribution of power would have. This is a difficult sentiment to explain to an American audience, which has been brought up in the rhetoric of democracy—although, as any cursory study of American history reveals, this country has *never* had a democratic government, nor was it intended to. The republican principles of the "founding fathers" were, to be sure, interlarded with lots of fashionable eighteenth century cant about freedom and brotherhood, but democracy was from the start plainly out of the question.

Still, Americans do not gladly hear that a writer of Nietzsche's prominence thinks so little of democratic principles.

To play devil's advocate for a moment, let us think of the nature of American mass culture at the present time and see whether there is any ground for Nietzsche's fears. The tragic art that Nietzsche praises may come from a primordial collective spirit and may therefore establish a link among all people. This Nietzsche does not object to; he is not opposed to the collective—quite the contrary. But the collective impetus he finds for tragedy comes out of the deepest desires and instincts of "the tribe." Tragedy, then, is popular art, or art that arises from the population itself. With Euripides begins mass culture, or the representation of ordinary people *from above* in an easily accessible way that makes no demand of them for their betterment, but instead praises them for being just as they are. Modern mass culture does precisely that. In Hollywood, rich producers and actors design an image of "ordinary Americans" for a situation comedy, and this image, imposed on the populace from above, reinforces the most ordinary aspects of ordinary people. It does not encourage them to grow or change or dissent—in fact, it exists to discourage thinking altogether, since a thinking population causes all kinds of problems for the ruling class in any nation, time, or culture. The objections Nietzsche (at least initially) makes against Euripides are largely of the kind that any partisan of popular culture would make against mass culture. Although, surely, Nietzsche could not have foreseen the devastating effectiveness of television as crowd control in the postmodern world, many of the darts he launches against Euripides here are not based upon contempt for democracy as an ideology so much as upon contempt for those who manipulate culture by praising its mediocrity. Least of all can Nietzsche tolerate what he regards as a cheapening of the stage of Aeschylus and Sophocles, those archetypal practitioners of popular culture—that is, the art of an entire people. To pander to the masses in this way, even out of a genuine love for them, is to do them an immeasurable disservice.

Nietzsche does not deny Euripides' talent and remarkable productivity. He only wonders why someone so gifted would choose to reconstruct tragedy in a way he finds inimical to its origins and traditions. Euripides is not the final scapegoat for the death of tragedy. Someone is in turn to blame for *his* subversion. There are in fact not one but two "mysterious spectators." One is Euripides himself, not as dramatist but as thinker. Nietzsche believes that Euripides demanded *understanding* from his experience of art and could therefore never tolerate the asymmetries, injustices, and irrationalities in the work of Aeschylus and Sophocles. Because of this, Euripides could not (Nietzsche speculates) comprehend the power of his predecessors. He needed therefore to turn to someone else for an explanation. And this was the particularly mysterious "other spectator."

Section 12

By this point in the reading of the text it should be clear that Nietzsche's style is not that of an ordinary German philologist. Using few examples and almost no scholarly references, he relies on a prophetic tone and a sense of momentum, rather than logical argumentation, to advance his thesis. The Dionysian is plainly irrational; but— and this is a more difficult point—so is the Apollinian. This is made inescapable enough by Nietzsche's constant association of Apollo with dreaming, one of the most unrational of human activities. But because of the fact that the Apollinian impulse generates individual heroes, figures long revered in myth and epic poetry, we may need to remind ourselves that the authority of these heroes is not based on reason. Even the inquisition conducted by Oedipus as he tries to find the cause of the plague is not rational. A reasonable person would have stopped asking such questions out of plain self-preservation. Besides, however rational the procedure Oedipus uses, what is revealed, of course, is the unreasoning hand of necessity (*anagke*).

One of the stylistic virtues of this book is that its principal theses and its manner of argumentation are entirely in harmony with one another. If logical argument has been assiduously avoided throughout, we may assume that Nietzsche finds something spurious in it. It is therefore not surprising to discover the identity of the "other spectator." It is as an allegorical figure representing reason itself that Socrates is introduced. And his rationality is just as hostile to Apollo as it is to Dionysus.

Nietzsche has been building considerable suspense about the identity of this "other spectator," and he teases us by not naming him until the third paragraph (the fourth in the Kaufmann translation). Euripides is first accused of having betrayed Dionysus. This may seem strange, since Euripides' *Bacchae*—really a kind of hymn to Dionysus—remains one of his most popular and powerful plays. It is also his last—and on this basis Nietzsche tries to explain it away. Here, at the end of his life, living in exile in Macedonia, Euripides casts a glance back over his career and regrets having sought to do away with Dionysus. Realizing his error, he writes one final play as a tribute to the god he has denied. In it he shows the young King Pentheus mad for order, determined to preserve the public tidiness of his land. Dionysus, in disguise, invades this realm, calling for the revels of his worship to begin. Pentheus orders him imprisoned; the god walks away and explodes Pentheus's palace with a wave of his hand. Gradually Dionysus casts a spell over Pentheus, creating in the monarch a desire to see those infamous revels (in which the rest of his family is already participating). The god promises him that a secret place can be arranged for his royal voyeurism. The one condition is that the king attend in drag, to blend in with the maenads. The embarrassed monarch is revealed to the revelers, who are hypnotized into seeing him as a stag. He is then hunted down and slain by his own mother. She carries his head back into town, and when clear sight returns the scene dissolves into lamentations. All of this proves the power of the god, who starts with the upper hand and retains it throughout.

It would be easy to interpret this frightening and powerful play in just the way Nietzsche suggests. There *is* an atmosphere of warning about it, a prescience of inevitable retribution if so strong a god is not given his due. And indeed there is as much superstition as supernature in the way Dionysus is worshiped. The play remains a favorite of psychological critics. It has protected Euripides from being branded by literary historians as a simple realist or rationalist. Its absence would make him look like a very different writer. Nietzsche was the first critic to write it off as an offering of mere contrition, having no relationship to the rest of his enormous output.

Nietzsche is now satisfied that the reader is prepared for his next and most daring accusation. He charges that Euripides wrote under the influence of Socrates, the Athenian philosopher immortalized in the *Dialogues* of Plato and in the *Memorabilia* of the historian-general Xenophon. Nietzsche offers no proof of any historical intersection of Socrates and Euripides, but the chronology and geography indicate that such a connection would have been *possible* at any rate. Socrates' dates are uncertain, but it is generally agreed that he was born before 469 B.C. and was executed in 399 B.C. Euripides was slightly older, living from 480 B.C. until 406 B.C. As usual, Nietzsche is not concerned with the factual value of his statement so much as with its metaphorical suggestiveness. Plausibility is all that he requires. Here is a new anti-dialectic, the Dionysian *and* the Apollinian versus the Socratic, leading to the death of tragedy.

One effect of this alleged Socratic influence is to prompt Euripides to abandon the Dionysian underpinning of tragedy, in order to establish a "dramatized epos." This is what some theorists (both before and after Nietzsche) have thought *all* tragedy to be: tidbits from Homer produced on stage. One of the principal aims of *The Birth of Tragedy* is to refute that view. But this is what Nietzsche thinks Euripides sank to, and implicitly he blames him for all such misinterpretations of tragedy.

Yet this dramatized epos, in which the playwright becomes in effect a replacement for the rhapsodist (the performer of epics), is different from traditional epic recitation in that it does not cultivate epic's cool detachment; in fact, it achieves a considerable rhetoric of passion (rather like the French classical tragedies of Corneille and Racine).

Here Nietzsche is making a concession to his scapegoat Euripides, admitting that there is *some* kind of emotional activity in his plays. Nietzsche protests, however, that this passion is not Dionysian, but merely the result of acting technique, of "fiery *affects.*" Similarly, what appears to be Apollinian is really the result of thought. Intellect has replaced Apollo, and method acting has replaced Dionysus.

These are grim charges, and given the literary reputation that posterity has conferred upon Euripides, they are controversial ones. To finalize his accusations, Nietzsche imputes to the Socratic the following dictum on aesthetics: "To be beautiful everything must be intelligible," following from the Socratic axiom "Knowledge is virtue." Plainly Nietzsche disagrees with this formulation. Throughout the remainder of his career, he argues against the existence of anything that could be called "virtue" or "knowledge" in any final sense. For Nietzsche, to say "knowledge is virtue" is as meaningful as a mathematician saying "$0 = 0$." The aesthetic pronouncement, however, the Socratic insistence on intelligible beauty, is taken more seriously. Much of Nietzsche's overall argument depends upon its refutation.

Oddly, he does not take it on directly. He leaves it to his reader to perceive the injustice of such a view. What is meant, simply, is that understanding of some kind must accompany the perception of beauty; that no aesthetic phenomenon can exist outside of some interpretive facility. Criticism, in other words, is indispensable for the reception of artworks. What Nietzsche calls the Dionysian, the modality that he finds essential to the very greatness of tragedy, is the diametrical opposite of this view. The beauty of the Dionysian comes primarily from its sense of *mystery*—the same mystery that causes wonder at the coming of spring, at the power of nature to regenerate after winter. Even the Apollinian, as Nietzsche describes it, devolves upon a mystery as profound as dreams themselves. What makes the Socratic so different from the Apollinian and the Dionysian is its need to *know* before it can respond to beauty. For the Socratic, the mystery cannot cause aesthetic fascination; only the *resolution* of the mystery can bring a sense of beauty in its wake.

The debate that such a remark might be expected to engender

continues to the present. In modern poetry, for example, Archibald MacLeish's lines, "A poem should not mean / But be,"[8] have provided a flag under which comprehension has been devalued as a criterion for poetic validity. T. S. Eliot said that the reader does not need to know what a line means to have some ineffable sense of its power. Leading contemporary American poets such as John Ashbery and James Tate have little interest in conveying meaning. Nietzsche is in the vanguard of those who argue that meaning is not the aim of art. Yet the idea that art ought somehow to instruct, or improve, or be true to life still persists today, though it is thought to be naive or politically extreme. The world Nietzsche was living and writing in believed, more than ours does, in such utilitarian rationales for art, and so his statement would have appeared more inflammatory at the time of its publication than it does today.

Nietzsche has split Euripides in two—into the dramatist on the one hand and the thinker on the other. It is Euripides-the-thinker who contrives the famous prologues and epilogues in which one of the characters, or (worse yet) some passing god, comes to center stage and gives all the information and other interpretive tools needed for "getting the meaning" of the drama. "Thus Euripides as a poet is essentially an echo of his own conscious knowledge." Euripides believes that mystery must be expunged from tragic art, even if it means destroying the integrity of the plot and the beauty of the illusion by such artificial devices as prologues and epilogues.

Sections 13 and 14

Nietzsche is not being arbitrary in branding Socrates an opponent of tragic art. From Plato's *Republic*, we know that Socrates would expel all the tragic poets from his ideal Athens. Why? In book 3 of the

Republic, he complains that tragedy does not serve an educative function for the army, as the Homeric epics possibly do. In book 10 the argument is longer and more complex. Socrates suggests that there are three levels in the reality of, to use his example, a couch: first, there is the Idea of the couch, which is created by god; then there is the actual couch, imitated from the Idea by a craftsman; then there is the image of a couch produced by a painter (who in this passage stands for all imitative artists). The artist is thus an imitator of an imitator.

> Then the mimetic art is far removed from truth, and this, it seems, is the reason why it can produce everything. . . . So we must consider whether these critics [who defend poetry] have not fallen in with such imitators and been deceived by them, so that looking upon their works they cannot perceive that these are three removes from reality, and easy to produce without knowledge of the truth.[9]

Socrates finds that such false representations are affronts to the gods, since the gods constructed the originals (the Ideas) that are being imitated at such removes. Artists are thus rather like unsuccessful would-be-gods, or false divinities. This is, Nietzsche charges once again, a judgment based entirely on the criteria of truth and knowledge, without regard for the mystery of beauty. It is good to remember, at this moment, Nietzsche's earlier assertion that the world is justifiable only as an aesthetic phenomenon, a phrase to which he will return again. The kind of power Nietzsche finds in tragedy is *truly* one that will be of no use in educating soldiers.

" 'Only by instinct': with this phrase we touch upon the heart and core of the Socratic tendency." The emphasis here is on the word *only*. Mistrusting anything but truth and knowledge, Socrates negates all that was wondrous in previous Greek art and culture, dismissing it as merely instinctive, hence as unenlightened and ignorant. An instinctive power like the Dionysian, as embodied in tragic choruses, is seen only as an interference to rational thought. For Socrates, intellect creates and instinct criticizes; Nietzsche believes that the exact opposite ought to be the case. Yet even Nietzsche is impressed by the single-minded,

subtly sublimated way in which Socrates pursues his dry goal of intel-
lectualizing the world. This is a perversion of passion, a passion di-
rected against passion itself. It explains the cheerfulness with which
Socrates went to his death.

There is also a political aspect to Socrates' banning of tragedy
from the *Republic*. This is the significance of the appeal that tragic
performances had for the masses of Athenians. The world of philos-
opher-kings that Socrates would have as his Utopia can scarcely be
expected to tolerate an art that does not appeal solely to the intellect—
for it is only the intellect that the philosophers can claim to monopo-
lize. Any other criterion for power would compromise their right to
rule. Tragedy is therefore mistrusted because it upholds the values and
traditions of the population as a whole, and discriminates against no
one as it generates its audience. Plato's abandonment of poetry for
philosophy, under the spell of Socrates, is indicative of the kind of
influence that Socratic thought would have upon literature.

Nietzsche, at this point, is still defending his proposition that Euripides was somehow secretly enlisted by the Sophists. He suggests
that Plato's *Dialogues* are a kind of drama recast by Socratic principles. "The Platonic dialogue was, as it were, the barge on which the
shipwrecked ancient poetry saved herself with all her children:
crowded into a narrow space and timidly submitting to the single
pilot, Socrates." In the war between the poets and philosophers, the
philosophers have won and taken the poets prisoner.

"Here *philosophic thought* overgrows art and compels it to cling
close to the trunk of dialectic." This once again recalls the opening
paragraph of *The Birth of Tragedy*, where dialectic reason as the sole
means of thinking is first attacked. Nietzsche accuses the heroes of
Euripidean tragedy of defending and explaining their actions. Worse
yet, he sees in the belief in logic a spurious optimism, the notion that
through contraries some kind of progress can be obtained. Tragedy, as
Nietzsche has described it, is beyond optimism and pessimism. The
Dionysian mode embraces suffering just as it embraces ecstasy, but in
so doing it does not deny the character or intensity of suffering. The
Apollinian mode is similarly ambiguous: individuation is a splendid

thing, to be sure, but there is also something good about the dissolution of the individual and the individual's reabsorption into Dionysian collectivity.

What is now called "this new Socratic-optimistic stage world" relegates the chorus, foundation of tragedy, to a vestigial survival and eventually destroys its music altogether: "that is, it destroys the essence of tragedy." Socrates may have a final vision of art that impels him, in his last days, to write a couple of verses. But implicitly, Nietzsche is comparing this late countermotion with that exhibited by Euripides in his authorship of the *Bacchae*. It cannot make up for the epidemic of rationalism that they jointly spawned in the prime of their careers.

Section 15

As Kaufmann's footnote points out, section 15 concludes the original version of *The Birth of Tragedy*. Most of the material concerning Greek tragedy is finished in this section, and what follows deals almost entirely with the dream of a *rebirth* of tragedy, again from the spirit of music, that is, from Richard Wagner. Meanwhile, this segment consists of another essay on Socrates. It is a very far-reaching speculation, with the kind of universal repercussions that characterize Nietzsche's later work. It is a bit of "skywriting."

"Like a shadow that keeps growing in the evening sun." This is Nietzsche's metaphor for Socrates' influence, even to the twilight of the present day. He has just accused Socrates of killing art; now he asserts that the prolongation of Socrates' influence will bring about "a regeneration of art." Sudden turns of position like this one are the dissonances in the orchestration of Nietzsche's thought, and they account for its particular beauty and poignancy. Yes, there is a trace of the dialectical synthesis: Dionysus against Socrates will yield ... something new, some new thesis. But at this point Nietzsche is really on his own. He is true to the aestheticist principle he framed so well in section 5. What he is concerned with is the survival, the "infinity of art."

He meditates on the tyranny of the past over the present, using the Greeks as archetypal examples of the problem. How can the present hope to achieve anything new when it is constantly haunted by the apparently inexhaustible creativity and versatility of Greek antiquity? For everything the modern artist contrives, Greek culture seems to have a superior example. Worse yet, the Greeks appear to have known that their place in the history of civilization was unassailable; they spoke as if it were. The charioteer metaphor brings this home in a depressingly powerful stroke: the Greeks hold the reins on all that follows, and most of the time the chariot and the team they control are inferior, worthy only of driving into the ditch. No wonder moderns resent the Greeks!

Is Socrates really predominant among these tyrants from the past? What is the nature of his influence and its continuing potency? Nietzsche argues that he is the original *theoretical man*. The distinction between artist and theoretical man is made, once again, with the aid of a metaphor. This time it is the covering and the thing covered. The artist takes delight in the covering by means of which the mystery is retained; whereas the theoretical man is concerned only with the act of uncovering. If science is concerned only with the thing uncovered, then it must be perennially unsatisfied; any totality of solution is not available. The mystery cannot be annihilated by any one person, even in a lifetime. Therefore the scientific (i.e., the Socratic) imagination gains its impetus from the *sensation of eternal progress*. This is why science so often finds itself in the company of positivistic ideologies, those that believe that we are always coming closer to complete truth about reality. Science has to believe in the "process of progress" because the product of complete knowing is forever beyond it. Nietzsche, who has up to this point found little to say in favor of the Socratic, now seems rapt with appreciation for the tragic implications of it all: the individual enlisted in the service of a species-long quest for knowledge. Where is there to go, when the inevitable failure comes, but back into a kind of collective identity: the scientists, the Sophists, the Fausts?

Nietzsche quotes the German critic Gotthold Ephraim Lessing (1729–81) to support the notion that it is the search rather than the result that obsesses science, its faith in the intellect's *ability* to penetrate and solve the mystery. This is a "sublime metaphysical illusion" that, like all illusions (even the Apollinian), reaches its limits. And there it encounters art.

The idea that the limits of intellect abut on art is a plausible but not commonly accepted one. The commonplace of our own age is that the outer boundary of science is religion. Einstein helped to promote this tenet when he attested that his journey to the edge of physics caused him to believe in God. The assumption is that his research yielded so much evidence of universal order that Einstein's *intellect* compelled him to believe in the existence of an architect of that order. Nietzsche bases his claim for art as the outcome of science on the myth (reported as history) of the death of Socrates. As Plato recounts it in the *Apology,* it has some of the flavor of a tragedy; critics have even seen this dialogue as especial evidence of Plato's suppressed dramatic gifts. Here is Socrates, so long the enemy of illusion, now dedicated to the illusion of absolute intellect and prepared to die for it. Is this dream of final truth really so far from that of Oedipus as he probes the mystery of the plague? "Myth has to come to their aid in the end"; that is, like all illusions, science must generate a mythology.

And so it has. The history of twentieth-century physics, whose desire for truth led it to discover the key to the very destruction of reality, would only provide more evidence for Nietzsche's speculation. Science ends in myth, all right. But not so much the myth of a dying Socrates as the myth of Armageddon, the dying of everything, and the eventual tragedy of consciousness itself.

After Socrates, Nietzsche continues, all philosophical schools are changed, all "Socratized." This is a kind of paraphrase of the truism that "All philosophy is a footnote to Plato"—yet another acknowledgment of the tyranny of ancient Greece. Now (to use Wallace Stevens's phrase) the "rage for order"[10] permeates everything, "actually holding out the prospect of the lawfulness of an entire solar system." As illusory as this fanatical pursuit of truth may be, it is better, according to Nietzsche, than leaving people without any overriding principle at all, abandoning them to pursue their own desires and eventually destroy themselves and one another through greed. Is this another foreshadowing of our own bloodthirsty century? Only art can prevent "genocide by pity"—that is, only art with its power to create myth can provide illusions powerful enough to allow people to believe that life is worth living.

The evil, the antithesis, is error. Or, following Plato's Socrates more faithfully, evil is stupidity, and unwillingness to examine. The desire to overcome such impediments to truth is the Socratic mind's greatest passion. Nietzsche believes that Socrates' optimism, based on a limitless faith in the power of knowledge, is the pivot of all the ensuing history of philosophy; all posterity has sought to vindicate this Athenian positivism. To complete its conquest often seems the only justifiable task of humankind. . . . And yet . . .

Again, what Nietzsche is *not* saying here is as important as what he is. The implication, throughout this rather uncharacteristically sympathetic appraisal of an enemy, is that *some force is emerging in modern philosophy that will finally end the rule of Socrates.* Nietzsche is assuming the graciousness shown by a conqueror to a defeated opponent. The aesthetic criterion will necessarily return to challenge the scientific one at last, after two millennia of Socratic domination. Science will come to wreckage on the patent logical impossibility of its own fulfillment. There will never come a time when all knowledge is secure. The metaphor of the circumference of a circle, breakable into infinities of points, shows that even when one reaches the theoretical limit of all that is knowable, smaller denominations of knowledge suddenly appear.

Think of particle physics, where every time a picture of atomic structure is about to be completed, another cousin of the quark or neutrino is discovered, or some other, even smaller entity appears. In

the face of this infinity, against which knowledge can make no definitive progress, a new, tragic, resigned Socrates emerges, a Socrates who
practices music, who is forced to go back to art *simply to preserve the
dream of order.* For if science cannot know everything, then all of its
accumulated learning is of no use. It cannot settle for shards of the
total structure unless there is a hope that the shards can someday be
pieced together into a whole. And rather than do without order altogether, a frustrated Socrates would sooner turn to art than to nihilism.

The "future history" that Nietzsche is toying with during the closure of this section is not merely a series of events that will come to
pass without human intercession, like the work of destiny, a *Weltgeist*
or world spirit. It is something in which even the individual must engage. Here the portion of *The Birth of Tragedy* that revolutionizes the
theory of tragedy ends. During what follows, we will see the philosopher "take part and fight." This will mean engaging in polemic.

Section 16

Nietzsche begins his polemic with the announcement that he is going
to concern himself only with the opposition of science and art, not
engaging other forces that oppose art at all times. One can only guess
at what he means by these "other antagonistic tendencies"—igno-
rance, nihilism, anarchism, or sheer barbarity, who knows? But his
first paragraph ends with the promise that new forces rising in the
world may bring about a rebirth (*Wiedergeburt*) of tragedy for the
"German being" (*deutsche Wesen*). (I am not sure why Kaufmann
translates *Wesen* as "genius" here.)

What is unnerving is the assertion that the rebirth of tragedy must
necessarily come in Germany. Why could Nietzsche not have made the
same argument for all of European culture? Or, like George Steiner in

his book *The Death of Tragedy,* dreamed of an extension of tragic art to whole new worlds, like China?

First off, Nietzsche is German, writing a book that issues from the German educational system; some ethnocentrism would be unavoidable, particularly in the wake of the Franco-Prussian War and the proclamation of Bismarck's empire. Soon enough, Nietzsche would take shelter behind Swiss citizenship to begin a lifelong attack on German culture and institutions; but not yet. The special bracketing of "German being" in this passage is a clue to the (often rather oblique) propaganda effort that Nietzsche is about to launch on behalf of Richard Wagner and his music.

Next comes a summary of the previous fifteen sections, ending in a citation of Schopenhauer's view of music from *The World as Will and Representation,* where that philosopher makes an extravagant claim: that music can represent *the thing-in-itself* or the Will directly. Perhaps this passage has been lurking in the wings of Nietzsche's book all along; perhaps it explains the primacy given to music in Nietzsche's account of tragedy's origins. Whatever the case, it is now out of the wings and onto center stage, and Nietzsche proudly credits it for what he already regards as the extraordinary insights of the first half of his book. Modesty is never one of Nietzsche's virtues, even at this early stage in his career, although he is still far from chapter headings like those in *Ecce Homo,* such as "Why I Am So Wise," "Why I Am So Clever," and "Why I Write Such Good Books." Throughout the remainder of his short life as a writer, he fell deeper into neglect with every book he published, so that without his gargantuan ego he would probably not have been able to persist, or write so well. Nonetheless, twentieth-century American readers are particularly well trained to dislike self-praise in an author (though they tolerate all manner of other egotisms), and passages such as these will always be hard to stomach.

A ponderous chunk of Schopenhauer follows, a long citation that, were this book an epic poem, might be called the "re-invocation of the Muse." Its point is that music is capable of representing the Will directly, whereas the other arts only imitate phenomenal reality in various ways. This places music in a unique position, as central as that of the entire faculty of representation itself. We therefore require some set of criteria other than the merely formalistic in order to evaluate music. "Delight in beautiful forms" will not suffice, since this constitutes an imposition of values from the visual arts. Music is in a separate and privileged category of aesthetics; some other vocabulary must be found to discuss it.

Music, according to Schopenhauer, is like geometry in that the forms it generates are not mere abstractions, but are "perceptible and thoroughly determinate." Feelings that come from the Will may be expressed through music without specificity, without the trivializing effect of a given plot, setting, or circumstance such as those that poetry, fiction, or the visual arts must use. Music does not reflect the phenomenal world in the same way as these other arts. Rather, music directly imitates the Will, the thing-in-itself, that mainspring of consciousness. If music is coordinated with "representative" art forms, it seems to lend them a particularly profound meaning, since they "both are simply different expressions of the same inner being of the world." (Cinematic scores appear to provide a strong modern corroboration of this point.) Such coordination cannot be achieved through reason or concepts, but only by some "direct knowledge of the nature of the world." Elaborating on Schopenhauer, Nietzsche suggests that, through this coordination with the other arts, music may give birth to myth in general, and the tragic myth in particular.

Here is a vulgar illustration of what Schopenhauer and Nietzsche mean: Music in and of itself may evoke images in the mind of the listener, even though the music is obviously not conveying the images directly. If the image of a lonely tower appears to me at the end of Anton Bruckner's Ninth Symphony, this is not because Bruckner wanted to convey such a picture; had he wanted to do that, he would have been a visual artist. The image in my mind is quite incidental under those circumstances.

Suppose, however, that the composer presents the music along with a picture, a text to be sung, or even a programmatic title to suggest what images the music is meant to induce. This would be an attempt to coordinate more than one art form. In that case, music lends an exalted quality to the image or text. Again, we have a more powerful example of this than Nietzsche ever had: movies. The intoning of French horns at the end of a western, while the hero rides off into the sunset, suffuses the scene with mythic grandeur. Similar musical mythopoeia takes place in other cinematic modes like science fiction, bootlegger movies, gangster films—all movies, in short. The union of music with narrative and image produces something greater than the sum of its parts, something closer to myth than mere representation.

Nietzsche is working on a secret agenda in this passage. Richard Wagner, also under Schopenhauer's influence, contrived to reorganize opera in such a way that music remains primary, while all other arts are included as well. This *Gesamtkunstwerk*, or "total artwork," was meant to generate myth by the union of music, painting (in scenery), costuming, dance, poetry, acting, and even architecture (since Wagner had his own theater constructed). His subject matter was Germanic mythology, and he believed that music could turn this mythology back into true myth. Wagner thought of himself as a modern Aeschylus. He believed that his theater at Bayreuth was destined to be the modern equivalent of the City Dionysia in antique Athens and that by reasserting the primacy of music and coordinating it with all the other arts, he would be able to bring about the rebirth of tragedy. Those reviewers who accused Nietzsche of "literary Wagnerianism" were aware that much of his discussion of tragedy is geared toward the revelation of Wagnerian opera as the successor to Greek tragedy.

The passing reference to Wagner in this section only hints at this, but it is a strong suggestion nonetheless. Wagner was noted not only as a composer, but also as an aesthetician; many of his writings on music and opera were enormously influential despite their obvious origins in Schopenhauer. Nietzsche is gradually edging into the realm of contemporary German art, but direct allusions to it will be reserved for later sections. In fact, section 16 ends with a particularly powerful restatement of the relationship of Apollo and Dionysus.

The question is, once again, why we experience elation in tragedy, why the destruction of a tragic protagonist brings a kind of joy instead of the more "reasonable" reaction of horror and compassion. Apollinian art maintains as its primary illusion the "eternity of the phenomenon," that is, the existence of ideal beauty as a counterweight to the suffering of human life. Phenomena, however, are not eternal, any more than the individuals who embody them. The hero "is negated for our pleasure," because in his or her annihilation we gain an affirmation of "eternal life." Even though a heroic character, full of beauty and ideals, is destroyed, in that destruction the Dionysian Will is affirmed. Behind the interminable flux of the phenomena and their incidental beauty, something more fundamental remains, something whose power transcends that of any individual hero. This is "the eternally creative primordial mother, eternally impelling to existence." Beneath the images of the world, there runs an unbroken music that builds myth and then destroys it, that spawns individuals only to draw them back into the whole. Tragic art is that which best illustrates this dynamic and accounts for the exhilaration we feel at what should otherwise be the uncompensated loss of an extraordinary individual in the tragic fall.

This notion of compensation is crucial for understanding tragedy in general. Without it, we would watch the blinding of Oedipus or the death of Hamlet either with stark horror or with sadistic glee. Without some counterweight of positive value, tragic art would be more or less what Schopenhauer simplistically says it is: the inevitable undoing of anyone who willfully engages with the world. This would be the most shallow sort of allegory. Nietzsche's contribution to our understanding of tragedy is enormous in this section. He is quite correct that in the fall of heroes something positive is implied. Oedipus finds a greater power than kingship; in *Hamlet*, Fortinbras ("strong-arm man") marches in to restore order to a world gone out of balance. Dionysus, cyclic god that he is, is a figure for this compensation. To say that all tragic personae are finally masks of Dionysus is to say that for every dismemberment a rebirth is implied. Tragedy is not the art of utter loss and grief, therefore. After the fall of an individual hero, a truer and more complete understanding, a kind of wisdom, something nearly eternal, survives.

Section 17

It is a "metaphysical comfort" that compensates us for the loss of the hero. This is perhaps why philosophers have traditionally placed tragedy at the apex of the arts, and why theory of tragedy has been more at home in philosophy than in literary criticism. Aristotle, in the *Poetics,* speaks of tragedy as arousing "pity and fear," but those emotions are readily compensated, according to Nietzsche, by our immersion in the oneness of being, once the individual is proven to be fragile and not eternal after all. The words of tragic drama alone, especially the speech of its heroes, do not suffice to make this metaphysical aspect immediately apparent. This is presumably because we cannot hear the choric music that was originally so important a part of tragedy. Left with words and words alone, the heroes may appear more superficial to us than they would have to their original Attic audiences. The musical part of tragedy must be reconstructed "by scholarly research," since it is obscured by later Greek art and philosophy that, as Nietzsche claims in his discussion of Socrates, have tried to suppress the Dionysian musical origins of tragic art. Dionysus "lives on in the mysteries," that is, survives only in various mystical religious cults, driven back underground—where he was before his legalization in Athens, the construction of the City Dionysia, and the birth of tragedy itself. But if Dionysus is merely underground, banished from cultural centrality by the new hegemony of reason, might the day not come when the god will rise again?

This depends on the continuing conflict between the *tragic* and the *theoretical.* The spirit of music and the spirit of science must be synthesized in "the music-practicing Socrates." Here is another example of Nietzsche's strategy of anti-dialectic, resolving what appears to be a logical contradiction by nonlogical means. After the submersion of tragic art by the coming of Socrates and science, degenerate forms of art resulted, among them the new dithyramb, a perversion of the original dithyramb, which was a hymn in praise of Dionysus. The late, decadent dithyramb does not try to reflect the Will, the oneness of being; it tries to imitate nothing so universal. Instead, it creates sounds that imitate superficial aspects of the words' meanings—a storm at sea accompanied by "stormy" music. This debases music to the level of mere accompaniment for the words.

Lurking beneath this passage is a historic debate that was raging between Richard Wagner and the critic, musicologist, and aesthetician Eduard Hanslick (1825–1904). Hanslick believed that music can convey no meaning in and of itself and that all "programmatic" music (i.e., music that aims to imitate some phenomenon, like the "Pastoral" Symphony or the "Ode to Joy") is imposing onto the purity of musical form a burden of meaning that it is not meant to bear. Hanslick was consequently a partisan of "pure" or "classical" composers like Brahms and Schumann, and a vehement opponent of Wagner, whom he contended was vulgarly trying to convey *meaning* through his music. Wagner in fact developed something called a leitmotiv (or "guiding motif"), a melodic or, in some cases, rhythmic fragment that is repeated throughout an opera (particularly *The Ring* and *Parsifal*) in association with some character, event, object, or emotion. The giants Fasolt and Fafner in *The Ring* have their own musical theme, but so do the River Rhine, the condition of Woe, and the end of the world. Hanslick objects to Wagner's association of music, that contentless medium, with such specific elements in the plot or with any specific phenomena whatever.

Nietzsche in this passage is covertly defending Wagner against these charges by repudiating (using the new dithyramb as emblematic scapegoat) all *directly* programmatic uses of music, all attempts to force music to serve words or stage effects. Implicitly, he is claiming that it is not a violation of the nature of music to associate a certain theme with a phenomenon, so long as that phenomenon (like an Apollinian hero) rises out of the music itself. If music remains primary, then any series of associations has the potential to become well-founded mythopoeia. The subtext here is that Wagner is not a programmatic composer as Hanslick charged, but that Wagner's belief in the primary and nonsignificating nature of music is beyond reproach.

This use of Greek history as a metaphor and analogy for German history is an aspect of *The Birth of Tragedy* that might easily be lost on a twentieth-century American reader. Nietzsche does not spell out the analogy as clearly as we might wish. Debates about these questions were passionate and even incendiary in their day, as events such as the *Tannhäuser* riot of 1861 remind us. Questions of culture—which may now appear to be minor points of aesthetic theory—were felt as urgent in a way that may be hard to understand now. Partly it comes from the fact that musical performance was still precious in the nineteenth century, since all music was performed live; there was no recorded music. To hear music required musicians! There was no radio, television, or other surrogate for performance that one could partake of at home. Music was a very public realm. This is no longer the case today, where through the use of earphones and a tiny radio or tape player a person can walk along the street with a concert hall between the ears—the ultimate privacy of the postmodern artistic experience, negating the entire rest of the world.

Furthermore, the public experience of art had to be shared with the artist, whereas with cinema, say, the round of applause the audience sometimes gives the screen at the end of a well-received film seems like an idiotic anachronism, since celluloid images cannot hear or come to center stage to take a bow. Twentieth-century art has been profoundly changed by technology, but in Nietzsche and Wagner's day the fundamental human desire to experience artworks was inseparable from the experience of being part of a community. Almost all of *The Birth of Tragedy* would have been read as an oblique manifesto of principles concerning the public, even political, way in which a culture consumes art.

As for the relationship of Greece and Germany, suffice it to say that Germany since the eighteenth century has thought itself to be in some special cultural relationship with classical Greece. Perhaps this is a result of the existence of early Germanic epics throughout Europe that seem to have a primacy for modern culture like that of the Homeric epics for antiquity. Or perhaps it comes from the fact that, after antiquity was "rediscovered" by the Italians during the late Middle Ages, Germany was quick to leap on the bandwagon, producing, generation after generation, the most eminent classical scholars and philologists. This is the tradition from which Nietzsche came, and which he was widely seen as betraying in this book. The Germans perceived themselves, throughout the nineteenth century, as the new Greeks, hoping to bring their culture to a pinnacle like that of, say, Attic tragedy. There is no doubt that Wagner regarded himself as a new Aeschylus, building his own version of the City Dionysia at Bayreuth and trying to re-create the cross-class popular audience that he believed Greek tragedy commanded. Because of the striking boldness of Wagner's claims, as well as Nietzsche's known personal connection to Wagner and his family, no reader of *The Birth of Tragedy* could have missed this now-obscured secondary level. As Wagner sought to play a role in modern Germany analogous to that of Aeschylus in Athens, so we begin to see that Nietzsche's tirades about the end of science and the transcending of Socrates are meant to contain a secret claim for his own succession to a similar philosophical preeminence.

Continuing to operate on these two levels at once, Nietzsche then broaches the matter of characterization in drama, beginning with a recapitulation of his argument against Euripides. After Sophocles, drama ceased to strive for mythic expansions of characters into eternal types, but instead sought through precise rendering of detail (realism) to develop only the individual (the phenomenon). In so doing, dramatists came to neglect the universal. This tendency is associated by Nietzsche with empiricism and the scientific method. He traces it from Sophocles to New Attic Comedy, but once again it is modern theater, with its catering to the audience's desire to see itself represented on stage, that Nietzsche is attacking. The subtext is that Wagner, whose characters are frequently drawn from Germanic or Celtic mythology, is on the right track, despite accusations from critics that his gods and heroes are pompous, stiff, and "unrealistic" (a charge still frequently leveled against him).

This unfortunate "new spirit" in art cannot offer any *metaphysical* solace for the loss of the hero, any compensation for the grief and horror of the fall. Earthly reconciliations are offered instead. The hero goes through a struggle of some kind, and then all conflicts are settled by events on the same "realistic" plane, rather than on any transcendental one. This is virtually a definition of comedy, where conflicts are negotiable and can be resolved without either the death of the hero or a revision in the world order. Euripides gets the blame for this. His famous prologues and epilogues are dismissed as dubious employments of the deus ex machina, the "god out of the machine." (This phrase, by the way, is funny but not as preposterous as it sounds, since *machina* refers specifically to the machinery used to control theater props. To show a god descending from the sky, for example, some variation on the block and tackle would be used. But the phrase still has a pejorative connotation, implying that easy, mechanical solutions are available for dramatic conflicts simply by pushing a button and dropping a god.)

The ramifications of this line of argument are complex. If Nietzsche is once again referring obliquely to himself as philosopher, then passages such as these contain implicit defenses of the method used in *The Birth of Tragedy*. For this book is incredibly short on detail, on illustration, on footnotes, quotations, or any other sort of documentation whatever. Here, in his own genre, Nietzsche is avoiding the "realism" (i.e., pretense to truth) that scholarship usually promises and is replacing it with mythopoeia—making new myths of Apollo, of Dionysus, of Socrates, and of the Greeks as a people. The resonance of such mythmaking is greater, in Nietzsche's view, than that of any solidly documented and detailed academic study, just as a well-wrought myth in, say, opera is preferable to the judicious and faithfully realistic rendering of a character.

This "layering" of meaning in the second half of *The Birth of Tragedy* provides a preview of Nietzsche's later critical technique, which often develops metaphors that may be read on several levels. Throughout his career he engaged in critical mythmaking, most notably in his character Zarathustra, but also in his myths of the Overman and the Eternal Recurrence, for example. Sometimes Nietzsche's principal value as a thinker is the richness of resonance that these myths generate. This is why interpreting Nietzsche is a risky, possibly futile, undertaking. Almost any exegesis necessarily limits the suggestiveness of the original text. Furthermore, this very suggestiveness may bring different things to different interpreters. Since Nietzsche contradicts himself so much, in the interest of attaining the maximum range of thought, his prose may be easily cited out of context to uphold all sorts of positions. This explains why Nietzsche was so vulnerable to expropriation by the Nazis, whose abuse of his ideas blackened his reputation for many years.

In any event, it is now apparent that in the second half of this essay he is allowing the unspoken parallel between Greece and Germany to ripen, until "Greece" becomes a kind of running metaphor for contemporary Germany.

Sections 18 and 19

Now Nietzsche classifies cultures as Socratic, Artistic, or Tragic. All of these are illusions, ways of creating a purpose in life for those higher spirits who are capable of sensing the horror of existence and who therefore need some kind of "stimulant" to survive. The Socratic offers the positivistic assurance that we will someday know everything that can be known and that we are making daily progress in that direction. Artistic culture provides absorption into the beauty of the phenomenal world, while the Tragic makes known the Dionysian wisdom that "eternal life flows on indestructibly." Now the parallel between Greece and modern civilization becomes explicit: Nietzsche describes the modern world as Socratic, or Alexandrian. Alexandria, a formerly Greek city now in Egypt, was the site of the greatest library in the classical world, whose burning (twice, actually, in 391 and again in 642) deprived us of any comprehensive knowledge of antiquity. The library is what first comes to mind when Alexandria is mentioned, and it is an apt symbol for an intellectual world that was custodial rather than creative. Science ruled, and the arts along with every other aspect of civilization fell under the schematics of scholarship.

Adherence to the Alexandrian mode is evident in modern myths. Faust, who vowed never to express satisfaction with any experience and who bargained with the Devil for the power to explore the outer reaches of knowledge, is the prototype of that modern hero. Yet the notion that Faust could even *imagine* (let alone fear) the limits of knowledge is already, for Nietzsche, an indication that the days of the scientific myth are numbered. What if science's cheerful tale of earthly fulfillment were taken literally by the masses? What if they rose up to demand it? Here Nietzsche is swiftly sketching in the development of socialism, with its optimism and belief in progress via the claim to scientific validity that Karl Marx provided for it. With the advent of socialism, Socratic culture may have engendered the very instrument of its own demise. A civilization of science and logic requires a slave class and uses mythology to maintain the loyalty of those slaves. With official myth and religion weakening, the myth of revolution (though Nietzsche never says this explicitly) may rise to replace them.

Kant and Schopenhauer are cited as heroic examples of men who, using the apparatus of science itself, attempted to discredit its optimistic claims to universality. I doubt whether Kant would have recognized himself in the role of a pessimist, although it is true that he declared final truth, the thing-in-itself, to be forever beyond the grasp of human understanding (although "reason" may still speculate about it). The description fits Schopenhauer to a tee, though, and Nietzsche predicts that these philosophers (implicitly including, of course, himself) have arrived to announce the end of scientific optimism and the impending rebirth of a tragic age. Socratic-Alexandrian culture, now sensing the end, fears most of all the coming of "the illogical" which will undo it once and for all.

At the start of section 19, Nietzsche plays another of the cards he has been holding for some time. He turns directly to opera and its history. This is a crucial moment for his argument in the book's second half: that tragedy will be reborn in the art of Richard Wagner. Here Nietzsche, for all his indifference toward consistency, does feel compelled to remain faithful to his *method* at least. He has argued that the nature of tragic art can be discovered in the study of its origins. And so he is compelled at this point to take stock of the very different origin of opera, lest he discredit the etiologic approach he used in his discussion of Greek drama.

In fact, there is cause for concern here. The birth of opera cannot be traced to the interaction of powerful and primitive gods. It is very much the product of an advanced civilization, coming into being at the very end of the sixteenth century. The High Renaissance had already passed and overripened. Even as Renaissance painting, however preoccupied with the human form, retained an ecclesiastical framework for its images, so too music had produced its greatest florescence in the context of the Church. Palestrina, whom Nietzsche mentions for the "vaulted structure" of his harmonies, is a good representative of this late sacred music. Medieval and Renaissance church music attached a religious value to harmony. That is, the playing of two simultaneous tones had not only a musical value, but an iconographic one as well. The perfect fifth, for example, represented the Grace of the Virgin, whereas the augmented fourth or diminished fifth was called Diabolus, or the Devil. Complex vocal works like Palestrina's were scored in such a way that the movement from one harmony to the next could be interpreted allegorically, the triumph of a God of order over the cacophony of dissonant demons.

The pioneering assault on this religiously grounded theory of music came from a group called the Florentine Camerata, which included the lutanist and composer Vincenzo Galilei (1520–91), father of the famous astronomer who would later encounter censorship and imprisonment for *his* repudiation of Church doctrine. The polyphonic style of Palestrina had reached its apex in the 1570s. In 1581 Galilei published a work of music theory, "Dialogo della musica antica e moderna" (Dialogue concerning ancient and modern music), which put forth his principles for a new and more expressive form of art. It was to be secular in orientation, looking back (in the fashion of late Renaissance "humanism"—meaning study of the Greek and Roman classics) to supposed principles of Greek music as a source for the

A Reading

reawakening of musical style. Claudio Monteverdi (1576–1643), the greatest composer and musical innovator of his age, published his first book of madrigals in 1587, and these works show the influence of Galilei's ideas. What is usually recognized as the first opera, *Dafne* by Jacopo Peri (1561–1633), came in 1594, three years after Galilei's death. Its subject, significantly, was drawn from classical mythology rather than Christian lore. Both Peri and another composer, Giulio Caccini (?–1618), staged operas called *Euridice* in 1600, and the following year Caccini announced an innovative vocal style called "Nuove musiche" or "New Music." Perhaps the first masterpiece of the new school was Monteverdi's *Orfeo,* which premiered in 1607. Word of the new union of theater and oratorio spread northward from Italy, and the first German opera, by Heinrich Schutz (1585–1672), also (and not coincidentally) called *Dafne,* was performed in Torgau in 1627.

The hallmark of this New Music was a curious manner of vocal delivery that eventually became known as "recitativo." In this style, singers vocalize in a middle-ground between singing and speaking, usually accompanied only by a keyboard instrument, though sometimes a string bass is added. This permits the singers tremendous flexibility, allowing them to move from speech to tonality according to the dramatic demands of the libretto. Recitativo survived to the maturity of opera, even through the middle works of Giuseppe Verdi (1813–1901), alternating with songlike melodic passages called arias. These distinct segments of operatic works—arias, duets, trios, recitativos, etc.—are called "numbers." Recitativo came to function as dialogue, the portion of the libretto that actually advances the plot, whereas the arias were primarily vehicles for the virtuosity of the singers.

Richard Wagner's most revolutionary contribution to the history of opera is his elimination, in his mature work, of numbers. Instead of alternating recitativo and aria, each of his "music dramas" is written as one continuous orchestral flow. The singing is rather like constant recitativo, rising from time to time into melodic passages that nonetheless do not have the tight opening and closure of traditional arias. Wagner thinks of the singers as boats floating upon the great sea of the orchestra. Some of this theory is lifted from Schopenhauer, but more important, for our purposes, it becomes the metaphor on which Nietzsche bases his speculations about Apollinian individuals (singers) and the Dionysian chorus (or orchestra).

How is Nietzsche to reconcile the very different origins of tragedy and opera? He begins with an evaluation of recitativo, asserting that it is a "superficial mosaic" held together by the contrivance of the librettist. He finds it so unnatural, so unlike either music or speech, that he places it outside both "the Apollinian and Dionysian artistic impulses," and seeks an explanation in some "extra-artistic tendency." At the same time, the Florentines who invented this hybrid style believed that they were somehow capturing the essence of the lost music of Greek antiquity. With ultimate "sentimentality" (in Schiller's specific sense of the word), they dreamed of returning to the "paradisiacal beginnings of mankind." This is the "extra-artistic tendency," then, a response to the powerful but nonaesthetic desire for primordial innocence. Nietzsche sees this as profoundly anti-Christian, as the expression of a need to discard the dogma of original sin in favor of a doctrine that postulates the continuing existence of Eden in human nature. He sees this as part of Renaissance humanism, the desire for a less dismal view of the human race than that provided by official theology.

This is seen as part and parcel of the Alexandrian or Socratic optimism that Nietzsche has already criticized at length. The rationalistic implications of this statement help to account for the domination of words over music in early operatic works. The real Dionysian passion that ought to inform true art is utterly absent. Here we see Nietzsche's snobbish side at work, since he interprets such a nonartistic art form as dangerously democratic, nostalgically primitive, liable to foster the damaging illusion that "every sentient man is an artist." This leads to a cheerfulness that Nietzsche finds frivolous, a far cry from the Dionysian cheerfulness in the face of suffering or the Apollinian "tragic joy" of an individual hero being reabsorbed into the Dionysian whole.

Here Nietzsche argues that a critique of opera necessarily entails a critique of all Socratic or Alexandrian consciousness. In other words, he gives opera a cultural centrality comparable to that of tragedy in ancient Greece. This is indeed what the Florentine founders of opera wanted to achieve, but Nietzsche is perhaps telescoping too many years of operatic history into a single glance. Even as he is apparently speaking of Renaissance opera, he is already talking about opera in his own century, where it did indeed attain such centrality. Still, for all the overcondensation of this passage, it does yield an important restatement of Nietzsche's idea of just what "true art" is—something very different from a flimsy hodgepodge of speech and song.

The function of art is "to save the eye from gazing into the horrors of night and to deliver the subject by the healing balm of illusion from the spasms of the agitation of the will." He thus demands a metaphysical basis for art, a foundation in human psychology that goes much deeper than the mere need for distracting entertainment, which obscures the horror only for a short spell. And Nietzsche, like Aristotle whom he opposes in so many other areas, is never in favor of unawareness. Aristotle's motto, "The unexamined life is not worth living," could be Nietzsche's just as well.

The superficiality of opera is due to the way it deploys music. Instead of being the original impetus for art, as in tragedy, music in traditional opera becomes "the slave of phenomena." That is, it responds to the "representation" of ordinary reality in the libretto. Associating Dionysus with music once again, Nietzsche sees opera as "the disappearance of the Dionysian spirit." But almost immediately, he tips his hand. He has been talking all along of *Italian* opera. When opera is unified with the great Dionysian(!) tradition of *German* music, then we may see the path opened for "the gradual reawakening of the Dionysian spirit."

The tradition "from Bach to Beethoven, from Beethoven to Wagner" is presented as a "demon rising from unfathomable depths" into the serenity and complacency of late Socratic culture. No longer is music merely mathematical. Here Nietzsche is obliquely referring to the tonal system, by which music was organized from the time of opera's birth until the late nineteenth century. The tonal system received its most comprehensive theoretical treatment in a work entitled *Gradus ad Parnassum* (*Steps to Parnassus*) published in 1725 by Johannes Fux (1660–1741). Without going into the technical aspects of counterpoint, suffice it to say that the tonal system is an extremely complicated series of rules about consonance and dissonance, and movement from one to the other. It is, as Nietzsche implies, a mathematical system above all, and not even the most elaborate and dense multiple fugues of Bach violate its regulations. The rules were bent for many years before they were broken, and even then they lost authority only gradually, with tonal works still composed well into the twentieth century. A great deal of credit (or blame) for the fall of the tonal system belongs to Wagner in opera, as it belongs to Anton Bruckner (1824–96) and Gustav Mahler (1860–1911) in symphonic music, and to Hugo Wolf (1860–1903) in the art song. It is possible to see such twentieth-century avant-garde composers as Igor Stravinsky (1882–1971) and Arnold Schoenberg (1874–1951) as reveling in the shards and ruins of a contrapuntal system that had stood for about three hundred years. Nietzsche is suggesting that the tonal system was in effect a Socratic harnessing of music, a forcible removal of music from its irrational origins to make it conform with the ruling principles of an Alexandrian age.

Nietzsche claims that German music is too powerful a force to be contained either in tight contrapuntal systems or in superficial operatic displays of "beauty." While it is true that Germany (with Italy) has one of the two greatest musical heritages in Europe, Nietzsche is stretching things a bit here. In a nationalist zeal that is far from the bitter anti-German diatribes of his later work, Nietzsche seems to be excusing German music from any complicity either in the early history of opera or in the domination of the tonal system. This is of course ridiculous. It is no coincidence that Fux, a German, codified the tonal system in its greatest completeness, nor is it accidental that the composer of the first German opera, Heinrich Schutz, became a student of Claudio Monteverdi. It *is* true, however, that in the nineteenth century German opera took on a dark brooding quality all its own. *Der Freischutz*, by Karl Maria von Weber (1786–1826), still the most performed opera in Europe, is deeply influenced by the disturbing supernatural fictions of E. T. A. Hoffmann (1776–1822), himself a conductor and composer, and by the folkloric research of the Brothers Grimm. Some of Wagner's early work, particularly *The Flying Dutchman,* plainly shows the influence of Weber.

What Nietzsche does in his account of the origins of Greek tragedy—creating a historical hypothesis—he does again in this passage. The details of German musicology do not concern him as much as the overall power of his hypothesis: that German music has somehow managed to keep alive the flame of Dionysian passion throughout all the centuries of Socratic domination of the West. He then adds two more ingredients, familiar ones in his recipe: Kant and Schopenhauer. Their attacks on the optimistic worldview of Socrates and science, coming along with the resurgence of German music, create the conditions for a rebirth of tragedy. To reach this point, history must move backward from a scientific to a Dionysian age. Such a backward motion, paradoxically, may lead to a revitalization of German civilization. "We can only inform ourselves by surmise from Hellenic analogies." On the *model* of the birth of tragedy from the spirit of music in ancient Greece, Nietzsche now predicts the coming of a new kind of tragedy in Germany.

Section 20

In this section Nietzsche conducts what can only be called a polemic. First he announces that the well-being of German culture shall be measured solely by the extent to which it emulates the civilization of ancient Greece. He recognizes past efforts to make such a rapprochement, notably those of Goethe, Schiller, and Winckelmann, but finds that these have fallen short of the ideal fusion of Greece and Germany that he envisions. He finds fault with those who have taken a purely historical stance, as well as with philologists ("dependable corrector of old texts") who mire themselves in the minutiae of linguistics. The professoriat has failed to address these eternal questions, taking its cue instead from journalism, which Nietzsche sees as hopelessly superficial and tied to the present moment. General culture and "true art" are far apart. How would so ephemeral a moment in history react to the rebirth of Dionysus and tragedy?

"Let no one try to blight our faith." How far such language seems from that of the earlier sections of the book. There the tone ranges from critical to prophetic and speculative. But all polemic implies some kind of "faith," and it is to Nietzsche's credit that he has the courage to trumpet it so directly. It is no wonder that he is hardest on these sections of the book in his backward glance from the end of his career; the whole concept of faith is one that the mature Nietzsche regards as anathema to his critical method. Here these pronouncements have a doubly hollow sound, full of ungainly nostalgia and, at the same time, full of a dubious certainty about the course of the future.

One of the dangers of studying antiquity is that we may catch ourselves sighing that the Greek world was passionate and luminous, while the modern world is by comparison venial and shallow. As Robert Fagles once remarked, "Certainly I love ancient Greece. But I also like my plumbing."[11] All Nietzsche's arguments about turning back from Socrates to Dionysus, about reversing history, might have been sustained if the prophetic tone prevailed, if its framework remained metaphorical. Nostalgia is facile in any circumstance; and here it is quite damaging to the overall intentions of Nietzsche's book.

There would seem to be no ground for Nietzsche's "faith"—save his faith in Wagner. This is again the subtext of this entire section: that Wagner will bring about the rebirth of Dionysus and that his opera will become the new tragedy. Indeed, Nietzsche's early relationship to Wagner was founded on blind worship and on a desperate need to be accepted by the master and his circle. Only when Nietzsche broke with Wagner did he become fully independent as a thinker; only then did he apply his usual critical method to the question of faith and the question of the decadence of modern culture. Not that he ever becomes pessimistic; he sustains his hope for the rebirth of civilization throughout his life, and he often uses Dionysus as a metaphorical figure for that rebirth. But his conception of Dionysus also becomes more complex. Certainly he detaches Dionysus from Wagner swiftly and definitively enough after the publication of *The Birth of Tragedy*.

In the last two paragraphs of section 20, he paints a picture of a transfigured world, where all the rubble of a dead culture is swept away in an apocalyptic firestorm. The tone of the final paragraph is familiar to those who have read *Thus Spoke Zarathustra*. There, however, the hortatory language is delivered through the medium of the main character, which allows Nietzsche to distance it. Spoken directly, as it is here, it makes the reader wonder on what level it is meant to be received. Surely not the literal: where would one get a thyrsus or find a tiger to lie at one's feet? The historical does not apply, nor does the ironical, nor even the prophetic.

At the start of section 21, Nietzsche asks how it is, then, that the Greeks, knowing Dionysus as they did, still mustered the conviction to form political states and fight wars. It is tempting to think that here Nietzsche is anticipating an objection from his German readers. Germany, like Greece, has a history of strong military activity. Will the rebirth of Dionysus in modern Germany negate that history and lead instead to "Indian Buddhism," that is, a quietistic end to worldly authority and war? Invoking Apollo once again, Nietzsche argues that the very existence of Dionysianism brings a counterforce with it, a resurgence of the *principium individuationis* that expresses itself in the formation of political institutions. The classical example of this reaction is the Roman Empire. This discussion is reminiscent of Hegel, who argued that the Absolute may sometimes be embodied in the state—specifically the Prussian state. This is one of Hegel's more disagreeable moments, and Nietzsche is not content to stop with it. Using "India" as a figure for a rejection of the world and "Rome" as a figure for the apotheosis of the worldly, he ascribes to the Greeks the development of a path between the two. "Here we must clearly think of the tremendous power that stimulated, purified, and discharged the whole life of the people: *tragedy.*"

Tragedy begins to emerge as an autonomous worldview, the greatest achievement of Greece, potentially renewable in modernity. It combines, as Nietzsche has argued before, the power of music with that of myth. The tragic hero relieves us of the burdens of nothingness and individuation at once—subsumes "India" and "Rome" into "Greece." This passage is something more than a recapitulation of earlier arguments about tragedy. Nietzsche is deliberately letting the concept of tragedy stray from literature into ethics and politics. He is developing the notion of a tragic worldview that is not bound by the stage, or even by the realm of art in general. It is a redemptive outlook, where even the destruction of the hero in his "greedy thirst for this existence" points to a higher order of being.

Whether or not "the tragic" exists outside the boundaries of literature is a question that has vexed theory of tragedy ever since Nietzsche. Some twentieth-century critics, notably Miguel de Unamuno, have tried to follow *The Birth of Tragedy* in establishing tragedy as an extraliterary philosophical weltanschauung. Less specifically, ramifications of this gambit can be seen in existentialism, particularly the work of Jean-Paul Sartre. The phrase Nietzsche uses with reference to the tragic hero, that he "takes the whole Dionysian world upon his back and thus relieves us of this burden," seems to have affected Sartre's idea of the existentialist hero.

The trouble with extrapolating from literary tragedy to a general worldview can be summed up in the following question: What becomes of the chorus? Nietzsche has argued throughout his book that the chorus and its music are the very cornerstones of tragedy. But if tragedy floats free of its literary origin and takes on the proportions of a general world outlook, then choric music is left behind. What then happens to myth, the sublime deception of heroism that emerges from music and creates the tragic totality?

Nietzsche retreats from the brink at this point and once again seeks his example in art: the third act of Wagner's *Tristan and Isolde.* He sees the tension between myth and music in Wagner "only as symbols of the most universal facts." This describes the method of the later sections of *The Birth of Tragedy*. What begin as ideas specifically about Greek tragedy are permitted to radiate into the most general areas of philosophy. Yet whenever the mechanism of tragedy seems about to be cut loose from literature and turned into a general scheme of things, Nietzsche returns to art for substantiation. In a sense, this is dodging the issue, but in another sense it is justifiable in that the *very existence* of tragedy within the context of a given civilization suggests certain things about that civilization's values. In effect, Nietzsche is having his cake and eating it, too. He is operating as if tragedy could be parleyed into an independent system and is permitting himself all the latitude that such a maneuver would afford. But by repeatedly returning to art, he sidesteps the morass of objections that would otherwise have to be answered, for example: What extra-literary equivalents of the chorus does modern civilization provide? Is *any* individual, purely by the fact of individuation, potentially a tragic hero? What is the nature of modern myth? How can tragic action be taken as a model for life, when tragedy is formal and life is not? To treat questions such as these would require a much broader study than this one. Nietzsche will in fact return throughout his career to "the tragic"; it is in his later writings that he will speculate more extensively on tragedy as the possible source of a worldview. Also, as with many such problems in *The Birth of Tragedy*, Nietzsche skillfully leaves the particulars to his successors in the field. Here it is again apparent that the purpose of this work is not to be exhaustive so much as suggestive.

The idea of the Apollinian as a healing illusion, presented much earlier and emphasized in these closing sections, suggests something about Nietzsche's attitude toward truth as the final criterion for philosophy. It is generally held to be the case that philosophers are above all seekers after truth and that their speculations are intended to make some sort of progress toward absolute knowledge. In his critique of Socrates, Nietzsche has already put aside all such positivistic notions of "progress." Here, though, we begin to hear intimations of an even more radical position. Truth alone may be lethal and can lead to pessimism, as it did in Schopenhauer's case. Nietzsche puts vitality, the life of the species, ahead of truth in his hierarchy of values. There are truths that kill (to paraphrase D. H. Lawrence), and lies that give life. The Apollinian individuation is just such a life-giving lie. Part of what would have been shocking to contemporary readers of *The Birth of Tragedy* is this apparently unphilosophic refusal to accept truth as the final value. For Nietzsche, transcending the tyranny of truth is part of the process of overturning the Socratic view of the world. Schopenhauer dismissed appearances as illusory and the Will as evil. Nietzsche is trying to preserve both, by reinterpreting the Will as the eternal Dionysian power, but also by refusing to reject appearances merely because of their illusory nature. This is part of the ongoing critique of Schopenhauer's pessimism, which Nietzsche would replace not with optimism exactly, but with a kind of tragic joy that embraces both optimism and pessimism as valid, and thereby transcends the dialectic.

"Internal expansion and illumination of the stage-world"—this passage, covertly meant to describe Wagner's work in "musical tragedy," also characterizes Nietzsche's method in these sections. Once again momentarily leaving his groundwork in art behind, he is exploring the ramifications of tragic art for life and philosophy. It would be very difficult indeed to make any sense of these passages without realizing that their real subject is Wagner. Yet Nietzsche, perhaps to protect himself from charges of literary Wagnerianism, perhaps to assure himself that he is writing for "those who know" rather than the uninitiated, mentions Wagner only in passing. Discusssing words and harmony, equating character and melodic line, he is championing Wagner's stagecraft. "Music is the real idea of the world." To dramatize character without music is possible, but in that case the character would remain "merely a phenomenon from which no bridge leads us to true reality, into the heart of the world." Nietzsche's procedure for convincing his readers of Wagner's claim to the cultural centrality of Greek tragedy depends on a kind of trick. Keeping Wagner in the wings, as it were, Nietzsche has gone on discoursing about tragedy *as if he were still speaking of ancient Greece,* using the same language and terminology as in the earlier portions of his book. The hidden message is that the mere fact that Wagner, scarcely named, can be spoken of in the same language used to discuss Greek tragedy constitutes in and of itself a kind of proof of Wagner's continuity with Greece and tragedy. In the following sections, Wagner is led somewhat more explicitly before the footlights.

Sections 22 and 23

Musical drama offers a much deeper kind of perception than the merely phenomenal. It allows a direct glimpse into the "thing in itself," the realm that Kant denied to the senses altogether and reserved for reason alone. Although Nietzsche uses Schopenhauer's term "Will," it is clear that he means to say that the greatest art affords a direct vision of the transcendental realm.

This cannot be accomplished by merely contemplative Apollinian art, which isolates and glorifies the individual in a timeless, plastic stasis. The art Nietzsche foretells is much more alive, a kinetic vision of the eternal motion of the Will. Aesthetics, ethics, and religion—Kant's triple road to the transcendental—are reunited in Wagner's *Gesamtkunstwerk* (total artwork) as they have not been since Greek tragedy.

The opening of section 22 manages to be doubly persuasive by an ingenious shift of focus. Now there is a new "third person," the "attentive friend." Nietzsche embodies this crucial argument in a new rhetorical format to make it stand out from what has preceded it, to emphasize its pivotal nature. The immediate purpose is to potentiate a description of the simultaneous joy and horror of tragedy, the simultaneous apotheosis and annihilation of the individual. Nietzsche is following Aristotle here, particularly the passage in the *Poetics* concerning pity and fear, and the *catharsis* or purgation of those emotions by tragic action.

The concept of catharsis is a difficult one, because it contains, as Nietzsche puts it, a "curious internal bifurcation," namely, that tragedy has the paradoxical power to arouse pity and fear, and then somehow to eliminate them. In other words, the hero's fall is not simply unmitigated horror. There is a counterthrust, a feeling even of calm, that ensues. Greek tragic trilogies were always followed by a so-called satyr play, a slapstick comedy often rowdy and sexually explicit, as is the only surviving example, Euripides' *The Cyclops*. From this fact it may be surmised that catharsis is a *structural* part of tragic drama. Modern theories of tragedy have generally treated catharsis as a psychological problem. Nietzsche, however, comes to the question with an advantage. He has already established a structural analogy for tragedy in Dionysus and Apollo. The complementary but also contradictory nature of these two gods, which Nietzsche has just finished reasserting, provides an immediate model for explicating the apparent self-contradiction of catharsis.

Aristotle's "purging" becomes for Nietzsche the moment in the emotional life of the drama when Apollo can no longer maintain the myth of individuation. Catharsis results from the fall of the hero, and this is the moment when tragedy fully realizes itself. All else hinges upon it. "The myth leads the world of phenomena to its limits where it denies itself and seeks to flee back again into the womb of the true and only reality." In reaching its limit, individuation perishes, reverts to its own contrary. As Robert Browning wrote, "What's come to perfection perishes."[12] Complete self-realization can only coincide with destruction (pace, Hegel).

Nietzsche accuses other critics of missing the point of the tragic fall, seeking its meaning in moral terms when it can be understood only from an aesthetic perspective. He quotes Goethe, asking whether it is possible to explain the "pathology" of the tragic as "merely aesthetic play" and answering in the affirmative. For this reason, Nietzsche does not consider another of Aristotle's enduring terms, *hamartia*, or tragic flaw. Moral explanations of tragedies always center on the "reason" for the fall of the hero. How did he or she overstep the bounds of what is right and proper, in order to bring down such a terrible fate? Needless to say, throughout centuries of Christian European culture this notion of a tragic flaw gets conflated with the idea of Christian sin. Such examinations of tragedy try to assign a moral

A Reading

explanation where, Nietzsche argues, only an aesthetic one such as his own will do. It is no one's "fault" that the hero rises and falls; the tragic fall is a direct result of the hero's extreme individuation in a cosmos where individuation is transient, where only the collective and anonymous can endure.

Nietzsche now contrasts the "attentive friend" with the critic, whom he blames for promoting the moral interpretation of art. "Incapable of enjoyment," the critic promotes in himself and others an interpretation "with half moral and half scholarly pretensions" that stands against art's real magic. The only emotions permitted by such critics are tied to extra-artistic matters such as politics or ethics. Their response to art is imposed from outside the artwork itself, whereas Nietzsche, still assuming that the world is justified only as an aesthetic phenomenon, believes critical intercession reduces art to a commentary on *something else*. This assertion is somewhat akin to later artistic dicta such as Archibald MacLeish's. Art must not be used as an instrument of moral indoctrination, or its real nature will be lost.

A test of one's relationship to art can be found in one's reaction to miracles represented on stage. Such events seem to deny realism and the mimetic "mirroring" of art. Critical intelligence is insulted by these things, but the aesthetic viewer accepts them as metaphorical, concentrated images. Myth, for example, cannot be taken by the critical mind without mediation of some kind, usually some form of abstract justification of the myth: Athena is the goddess *of wisdom* because it is not sufficient that she be simply a goddess. Nietzsche believes that no culture can maintain its vitality without taking its myths full strength, undiluted with moral concerns. He finds this moralizing to be rampant in modern Europe and believes that there is no hope for the resurgence of culture unless myth is restored in all its original luminousness. (Again, it is necessary to bear in mind that he is still making a brief for the mythologically grounded art of Richard Wagner.)

Hope for the rebirth of Germany may stem from the predominance of music in that country's history. Nietzsche is perhaps stretching our credulity when he compares the austere chorales of Martin Luther with "the first Dionysian luring call breaking forth from dense thickets at the approach of spring," but the fact remains that Germany (along with Italy) does possess one of the two greatest musical cultures in Europe. Only the ever-present example of ancient Greece, however, will suffice for empowering Germany's mythic rebirth. Only in the light of this antique world can mythic timelessness be achieved, a glimpse of eternity that transcends the ephemeral quality of daily life and quotidian culture.

This passage, with its naive cultural nationalism, is one of the few that seem to serve the Nazi revision of Nietzsche. There is no doubt that Wagner and Nietzsche, with their theories of myth, provided Hitler with inspiration for the elaborate staging of his Nuremberg rallies in the 1930s. There is such a thing as a myth of the mythic, which can be slanted for political purposes. Nearly every successful politician engages in mythopoeia to some extent; advertising campaigns are another modern equivalent. The trouble with the glorification of Germanic myth in this way is that it suggests that Germany is the *exclusive* heir to Greece. Along with his few instances of anti-Semitism, Nietzsche left chauvinism behind as he matured. The misuse of Nietzsche by the Nazis is like any other form of political expropriation: it takes what it wants and leaves the rest in obscurity, citing passages out of context, reinterpreting broad problems from narrow perspectives.

With the close of section 23, the main argument for the rebirth of tragedy in modern Germany is completed, and Nietzsche is now ready for summation.

Sections 24 and 25

Throughout *The Birth of Tragedy,* the reader may be surprised by the enormous importance Nietzsche allots to art in the total picture of civilization. The mass culture of our age, like that of Nietzsche's, is ephemeral, prey to rapid changes of fashion and an insatiable appetite for the new. In our age the centrality of *any* art, last manifested in 1960s rock music and cinema, has been replaced by the centrality of video. Whether video is an art form is a moot point; it is a medium, like sculpture or opera, and can be used to create either art or mere distraction. If we look around for the central art form of our day, one that approximates the dominance of opera or painting or the novel in the nineteenth century, we are at a loss. Presumably the various forms of television serve the function of replacing art. And, as Andy Warhol's soup cans in museums taught us, whatever takes the place of art *becomes* art. As the philosopher Arthur Szathmary once remarked, to call something art is not to make a value judgment about it. Like cinema, television combines music, dance, drama, and the visual arts into a modern *Gesamtkunstwerk,* or "total artwork," to use Wagner's term. While its cultural effects may be deplorable, it must be admitted that video possesses a kind of social centrality unimaginable in the nineteenth century.

Wagner may be seen as a predecessor of cinema and television. He envisioned a spectacle, made up of all the arts, that would draw its audience from all social classes and regions of his country. Nietzsche's break with the Master may be traced, in fact, to the opening night of the theater at Bayreuth that Wagner intended to be the modern equivalent of the City Dionysia in Athens. Nietzsche was horrified at the wealthy and complacent audience that Wagner's spectacle attracted. Certainly Wagner never dreamt of an "art" that could pursue the audience right into their homes; but, if he had been able to, such a dream would probably have enthralled him. He was nevertheless working with all the arts *out of the tradition of a single one—* opera. And opera was and is hopelessly confined to the taste of the wealthier and better-educated classes.

The same was not true of Attic tragedy, which appealed to all of the Athenian population. It is hard for us to imagine art of such seriousness attracting any but the educated and affluent; we think of tragedy and opera now as "high culture." But in the early 1870s the dream of re-creating high art for the masses was not as preposterous as it is today. Wagner's plan for a "total artwork" was immensely exciting and aroused the partisanship of many artists and critics besides Nietzsche. It also incurred the most passionate animosity, which is testimony to the composer's truly radical vision.

True, history has found that Wagner's preoccupation with mythology, which Nietzsche thinks is the heart of his claim to modern tragedy, makes his operas rather wooden and inhuman. His adaptation of the recitativo now seems pompously declamatory, and his vaunted libretti are weighed down with rehashed Schopenhauer and other tedious disquisitions. Only in the confines of *music* history does Wagner's place seem secure. His contribution to orchestration is crucial, as is his audacity in dismantling the tonal system.

Nietzsche's excessive devotion to Wagner is understandable both as a psychological fact of Nietzsche's youth and as a historical phenomenon. As *The Birth of Tragedy* comes to a close, the summations seem almost breathless with enthusiasm. The relationship between Apollo and Dionysus is rehearsed again. True to his opening paragraph, Nietzsche does not make a logical synthesis between them. Rather, he sees each enhancing the other in tragic art and in the creation of tragic myth. Each god, in symbiosis with the other, becomes more than what he was. Apollo no longer need settle for sculpture and musicless drama, and Dionysus need no longer settle for formless orgies of dancing.

Nietzsche expresses his belief in the centrality of art with a brilliant phrase: "Art is not merely imitation of the reality of nature but rather a metaphysical supplement of the reality of nature, placed beside it for its overcoming." This sentence leads to the repetition of the famous phrase from section 5, "that existence and the world seem justified only as an aesthetic phenomenon." Speaking strictly in musical terms, Nietzsche associates Dionysus with dissonance, as he associates Apollo with consonant harmony. Music that is only consonance could never be as aesthetically complete as music that contains both consonance and dissonance. This line of argument echoes on several levels of the book as a whole.

First, it is yet another covert defense of Wagner, whose revolutionary harmony and orchestration struck many nineteenth-century listeners as painfully dissonant. But it is also a foreshadowing of another of Nietzsche's principal doctrines, one that he would make much of throughout his career and would later explicitly call "The Dionysian." This is the capacity for suffering itself, and a love of fate that permits us to see suffering as a legitimate part of life, as much as pleasure and exaltation. Third, it is an argument for a "tragic view of life" that Nietzsche finds preferable to the cheerful and shallow positivism of his day and to the materialistic claims and hypotheses of socialism. Nietzsche's position on suffering bears some resemblance to romantic views, such as that of John Keats, who argued for "negative capability," or the tolerance of contradictions that permits the acceptance of suffering.

Nietzsche would never again articulate so aestheticist a view of the world. But in so doing he is really not all that far from Immanuel Kant, who in the *Critique of Judgment* stated that "Nature is beautiful because it looks like art." In both philosophers' cases, these aestheticist statements must be taken in context. Taken by themselves, they sound like ammunition for the Decadent writers at the century's end. Kant intended his statement to mean that when we perceive beauty in nature, we impute to it a sense of formal awareness, what he called "purposiveness without a purpose." Similarly, Nietzsche must be understood to be positing his aestheticism in the spirit of another bit of John Keats: " 'Beauty is truth, truth beauty,'—that is all / Ye know on earth, and all ye need to know."[13] What Nietzsche is really doing is calling for the replacement of *scientific* truth with aesthetics. He believes this to be the first criterion of human life, deep in Greek antiquity, an ideal way of reading the world that we have fallen away from, and to which we should return.

As such, it is still partly a metaphor. Music, as he says toward the end of the section, has a close relationship with myth—Dionysus generating Apollo. When Nietzsche invokes the slumbering German giant beneath the earth, it is again reminiscent of a romantic forebear: William Blake's dream of awakening the sleeping giant Albion (England). It is fascinating to see Nietzsche still in the thrall of romantic ideas and, especially in these later sections of his book, romantic rhetoric. The older Nietzsche will have a greater role than almost anyone else in dethroning romanticism, at least from one part of its vast kingdom of influence.

Here, however, he concludes with a reaffirmation of the uncharacteristic "faith" announced earlier. It is the uncritical nature of passages like this that eventually led Nietzsche to renounce, more or less, the second half of his book.

6

CONCLUSION

The Birth of Tragedy is an ambitious book. It has as its goal a change in consciousness itself, and the reawakening of a civilization. Like all truly revolutionary works, it needs to revise history in order to create the future. Nietzsche's version of the origin and demise of Greek tragedy is precisely that sort of rewriting of the past, and this, if nothing else, it has in common with other radical texts like *Das Kapital, The Origin of Species,* and all the works of Freud. Its importance lies not in any one of the several disciplines it tries to integrate, but in that most general and fundamental of all interdisciplines, the history of consciousness.

True, the book *is* meant to erect a historical scaffolding for the art of Richard Wagner and for the cultural upheaval that Nietzsche thought would come in Wagner's wake. In my view, this does not damage the work's integrity. Wagner, after all, was and is eminently worthy of attention. Time has vindicated him, more or less. His place in operatic history is secure, and his works are still performed in Bayreuth and every great house on earth. His art was not, at last, radical enough to change consciousness and the world; but it did change the arts forever. Still, it did not finally confront the bourgeois society Nietzsche hated so much; nor did Bayreuth reunify the German-speaking nations; nor did Dionysus rise from the soil to walk on earth again. Nietzsche turned against Wagner before long. At Wagner's death in 1883, six years after Nietzsche split with him, the disillusioned philosopher said he was "vastly relieved."

Perhaps *The Birth of Tragedy* contributed in some measure to Wagner's success; probably Wagner would have prevailed anyway. In any case, Nietzsche's partisanship of the composer is no longer an urgent matter. It is the first half of *The Birth of Tragedy* that exerts the greater continuing influence.

Debate still rages over Nietzsche's account of the origin of tragedy, with his detractors usually outnumbering his supporters. Because of the lack of documentation and relevant evidence in *The Birth of Tragedy,* its theories are left wide open for attack. While the importance of Dionysian religion for the founding of tragic performance has gained some acceptance, there are still those who believe that tragedy is really a more or less direct dramatization of epic poetry, accompanied by a bit of music and dance. Gerald Else, for example, who admires Nietzsche even while disagreeing with him, sees the tyrant Solon as the moving force in the creation of tragedy. There is a certain "your guess is as good as mine" quality to all these speculations. Attic tragedy is so complex a form of drama that it is difficult to think that it would not have incorporated elements from the entire range of Greek life and thought into its texture, as did the epic before it. The disagreements of scholars are often questions of emphasis: which input was most important? And because so much of antiquity is forever hidden from us, after the burning of the library at Alexandria, the "truth" (to use Nietzschean quotation marks) may never be fully known.

Delivering the verdict on *The Birth of Tragedy* using factual or historical criteria is a misdirected effort. It is enough to say that for several decades the book injected new enthusiasm into the work of classical scholars, regardless of whether their findings agree with Nietzsche's speculations or not. Nietzsche's manipulation of history may have its basis in, once again, the work of Ralph Waldo Emerson. One of Emerson's essays, "History," certainly known to Nietzsche, makes a case for history as a process of consciousness rather than just a march of facts and events. History, according to Emerson, is a manifestation of the Oversoul, or Absolute spirit. Part of the opening of the essay reads:

> There is one mind common to all individual men. Every man is an inlet to the same and all of the same. . . . Who hath access to this universal mind is a party to all that is or can be done, for this is the only and sovereign agent.
>
> Of the works of this mind history is the record. . . . But thought is always prior to the fact; all the facts of history pre-exist in the mind as laws.[14]

If *The Birth of Tragedy* is recognized as an example of Emersonian history, then it becomes clear that Nietzsche is consciously turning away from a documented and factual kind of history—the nuts and bolts of philology—toward history of consciousness. This book is not intended to transmit the last word on Greek tragedy. It is meant to stimulate further speculation, and in this regard it succeeds admirably.

As far as its impact on philosophy is concerned, it is hard to assess the influence of *The Birth of Tragedy* apart from the rising and falling fortunes of Nietzsche's oeuvre as a whole. Most philosophers do not think much of it in and of itself. Some regret the partisanship of its second half, others the imprecision of its vocabulary, others the often unsatisfying form of its argumentation. Some, including the older Nietzsche, think it too close to Schopenhauer. The attack on Socrates, however, is a landmark in modern antirationalism. Broadside assaults on reason were anything but common in the positivistic climate of the mid-nineteenth century. Irrationalism had been for some time confined to theology and literature. The great middle-class revolutions of the late eighteenth century had been waged in the name of reason, as had the overthrow of older theocentric philosophical systems in favor of post-Kantian forms of humanism.

It is true that the medium through which Nietzsche begins his lifelong war against reason is somewhat suspect. The significance he gives to the influence of Socrates on Euripides has no historical ground whatever, nor can Socrates (whose prestige in his own time was negligible) realistically be blamed for the death of tragedy, which simply reached its zenith and declined. All such moments of extraordinary artistic achievement are brief; the Italian High Renaissance in painting lasted all of twenty years, for example, and Shakespeare's career was barely longer than that. Socrates, like Dionysus, keeps turning up as a "character" in Nietzsche's writing from *The Birth of Tragedy* onward. During his middle period, Nietzsche treats him with something like reverence, only to renew his attacks toward the end. Still, it is easy to see the concatenations of this initial assault reverberating through dadaism, surrealism, existentialism, futurism, (alas) fascism, and even the libertarian countercultural uprising in America in the 1960s.

Like his mentor Schopenhauer, Nietzsche is one of the few philosophers whose literary influence has been as great as or even greater than his impact on philosophy. Many poets in many languages have been moved by the idea of an early Dionysian art and the prospect of its rebirth. The Irish poet William Butler Yeats (1865–1939), in his mystical system expounded in *A Vision*, sees the world in alternating cycles of the solar and the lunar, the primary and the antithetical. Nietzsche's Dionysus is plainly the model for the antithetical, the anti-Christian "rough beast, its hour come round at last" who "slouches toward Bethlehem to be born."[15] In the work of the French symbolist poet Stephane Mallarmé (1842–98), a faun creates momentarily and provisionally individuated nymphs out of the reservoir of his erotic desire; when his dreaming stops, the nymphs fade back into the shadows. In "Hérodiade" a brittle, overindividuated princess tries desperately to cling to a kind of Apollinian illusion while spirits of old warriors lie in the basement of her castle in their unquiet graves. The German mystical poet Rainer Maria Rilke (1875–1926) uses the figure of Apollo frequently; Stefan George (1868–1933) wrote two important poems about Nietzsche; and Gottfried Benn (1886–1956) wrote a late essay acknowledging Nietzsche's importance in his work.

This is a very incomplete list, but it is even more difficult to give a comprehensive assessment of the influence of *The Birth of Tragedy* on fiction. In some measure, the modernist indictment of culture and civilization rises out of the combined impact of Nietzsche and Freud. *L'Immoraliste* (*The Immoralist*), the first novel of André Gide (1869–1951), published in 1902, is full of Nietzschean ideas drawn from all the philosopher's work, but what is drawn from *The Birth of Tragedy* specifically is the notion that Dionysian intoxication still lives in its country of origin, north Africa. Michel, Gide's protagonist, turns against French culture and his own academic background, and ends up in a desert hovel, stripped of his identity and intoxicated with sensual life. The same myth recurs in *The Sheltering Sky*, a novel published in 1949 by the American expatriate Paul Bowles (b. 1911), where an American woman traveling in north Africa discovers a dark erotic power that forever prevents her return to civilized existence.

Thomas Mann (1875–1955), the great German novelist who was also an accomplished student of philosophy, particularly of Schopenhauer and Nietzsche, shows the influence of *The Birth of Tragedy* explicitly in his 1911 novella *Der Tod in Venedig* (*Death in Venice*), where a cholera plague from the East invades Venice. Gustave von Aschenbach, the protagonist, is a northerner, a novelist whose work is particularly dear to "official culture" and whose personality is said to be based upon the asceticism of the composer Gustav Mahler. Von Aschenbach, after seeing a mysterious foreigner in a Munich cemetery, decides to take a vacation. During his sea-voyage into Venice, he sees a Silenus-like character, the "young-old man" reveling with younger men, "deplorably drunk," as the moralistic Aschenbach thinks. Like Gide's Michel, Aschenbach finds himself suddenly open to homosexual impulses, falling in love with a young Polish tourist named Tadzio. As the plague advances upon the city, it develops into a metaphor for death and sexuality taken together. Lingering in the city because of his intoxication with the boy, Aschenbach falls victim to the plague in both senses, experiencing a sexual awakening just before his death.

Von Aschenbach has a dream that is worth reproducing in its entirety, since it is such a splendid dramatization of what Nietzsche means by the Dionysian. The following is the translation of H. T. Lowe-Porter:

The beginning was fear; fear and desire, with a shuddering curiosity. Night reigned, and his senses were on the alert; he heard loud, confused noises from far away, clamour and hubbub. There was a rattling, a crashing, a low dull thunder; shrill halloos and a kind of howl with a long-drawn *u*-sound at the end. And with all these, dominating them all, flute-notes of the cruellest sweetness, deep and cooing, keeping shamelessly on until the listener felt his very entrails bewitched. He heard a voice, naming, though darkly, that which was to come: "The stranger god!" A glow lighted up the surrounding mist and by it he recognized a mountain scene like that about his country home. From the wooded heights, from among the tree-trunks and crumbling moss-covered rocks, a troop came tumbling and raging down, a whirling rout of men and animals, and overflowed the hillside with flames and human forms, with clamour and reeling dance. The females stumbled over the long, hairy pelts that dangled from their girdles; with heads flung back they uttered loud hoarse cries and shook their tambourines high in air; brandished naked daggers or torches vomiting trails of sparks. They shrieked, holding their breasts in both hands; coiling snakes with quivering tongues they clutched about their waists. Horned and hairy males, girt about the loins with hides, dropped heads and lifted arms and thighs in unison, as they beat on brazen vessels that gave out droning thunder, or thumped madly on drums. There were troops of beardless youths armed with garlanded staves; these ran after goats and thrust their staves against the creatures' flanks, then clung to the plunging horns and let themselves be borne off with triumphant shouts. And one and all the mad rout yelled that cry, composed of soft consonants with a long-drawn *u*-sound at the end, so sweet and wild it was together, and like nothing ever heard before! It would ring through the air like the bellow of a challenging stag, and be given back many-tongued; or they would use it to goad each other on to dance with wild excess of tossing limbs—they never let it die. But the deep, beguiling notes of the flute wove in and out and over all. Beguiling too it was to him who struggled in the grip of these sights and sounds, shamelessly awaiting the coming feast and the utmost surrender. He trembled, he shrank, his will was steadfast to preserve and uphold his own god against the stranger who was sworn enemy to dignity and self-control. But the mountain wall took up the noise and howling and gave it back manifold; it rose high, swelled to a madness that carried him away. His senses reeled in the steam of panting bodies, the acrid stench from the goats, the odour as of stagnant waters—and another, too familiar smell—of wounds, uncleanliness and disease. His heart throbbed to the drums, his brain reeled, a blind rage seized him, a whirling lust, he craved with all his soul to join the ring that formed about the obscene symbol of the godhead, and they were unveiling and elevating, monstrous and wooden, while from full throats they yelled their rallying-cry. Foam dripped from their lips, they drove each other on with lewd gesturings and beckoning hands. They laughed, they howled, they thrust their pointed staves into each other's flesh and licked the blood as it ran down. But now the dreamer was in them and of them, the stranger god was his own. Yes, it was he who was flinging himself upon the animals, who bit and tore and swallowed smoking gobbets of flesh—while on the trampled moss there now began rites in honour of the god, an orgy of promiscuous embraces—and in his very soul he tasted the bestial degradation of his fall.[16]

There is no better explication of *The Birth of Tragedy.*

This commentary has endeavored to expose certain recurrent themes, images, and ideas of Nietzsche's text. But the book's survival as a powerful influence on the thought of our own century is due largely to the *emotional* implications of what it says. When Nietzsche's seeds fall upon art, in later writers, they grow into powerful idea-images that stir the unconscious deeply and unforgettably. Nietzsche came to believe more and more, in the course of his short career, that ideas can never be divorced from their emotional content; that there is no such thing as "pure" intellection, thought into which the heart does not enter. As a work of philosophy, the book has many faults. As a work of philology, it is in *de*fault. As history it fails for lack of factual foundation. But as that most vital kind of book—a work of consciousness itself—it holds in our history an immutable and precious place.

NOTES

1. *Ecce Homo*, trans. Walter Kaufmann (New York: Random House, 1976), 270; hereafter cited in the text.

2. Dylan Thomas, *Collected Poems* (London: J. M. Dent and Sons, 1952), 9.

3. George Thomson, *Aeschylus and Athens* (New York: Grosset and Dunlap, 1968), 103–4.

4. Arthur Schopenhauer, *The World as Will and Representation*, trans. E. F. J. Payne (Indian Hills, Colo.: Falcon's Wing Press, 1958), 18.

5. Ibid., 100.

6. Ibid., 253.

7. Ezra Pound, *The Cantos of Ezra Pound* (New York: New Directions, 1948), 59.

8. Archibald MacLeish, *Poems, 1924–1933* (New York and Boston: Houghton Mifflin, 1933), 123.

9. Edith Hamilton and Huntington Cairns, eds., *The Collected Dialogues of Plato* (New York: Bollingen, 1961), 823–24.

10. Wallace Stevens, *Collected Poems* (New York: Alfred A. Knopf, 1965), 130.

11. A remark made to the author.

12. Robert Browning, *The Poems* (New Haven and London: Yale University Press, 1981), 1:660.

13. John Keats, "Ode on a Grecian Urn," in *The Poetical Works and Other Writings* (New York: Phaeton, 1970), 3:157.

14. Ralph Waldo Emerson, *Essays: First Series* (Boston and New York: Houghton Mifflin, 1903), 3.

15. W. B. Yeats, *Collected Poems* (New York: Macmillan, 1956), 185.

16. Thomas Mann, *Death in Venice*, trans. H. T. Lowe-Porter (New York: Knopf, 1936), 67–68.

BIBLIOGRAPHY

Primary Sources

German Editions

Hegel, G. W. F. *Sämtliche Werke*. Edited by Hermann Glockner. 20 vols. Stuttgart: Frommann, 1927–30.

Nietzsche, Friedrich, *Grossoktavausgabe*. Edited by Elisabeth Förster-Nietzsche et al. 2d ed. Leipzig: Kröner, 1901–13.

———. *Gesammelte Werke, Musarionausgabe*. Munich: Musarion Verlag, 1920–29.

———. *Werke, Kritische Gesamtausgabe*. Edited by G. Colli and M. Montinari. Berlin and New York: De Gruyter, 1967–.

———. *Gesammelte Briefe*. Edited by Elisabeth Förster-Nietzsche et al. Leipzig: Kröner, 1900–1909.

Schiller, F. *Sämtliche Werke*. 5 vols. Munich: Winkler, 1968.

Schopenhauer, Arthur. *Sämtliche Werke*. Edited by Wolfgang Frhr. von Löhneysen. 5 vols. Stuttgart: Cotta und Insel, 1960–65.

Wagner, Richard. *Sämtliche Schriften und Dichtungen*. 12 vols. Leipzig: Breitkopf und Härtel, 1911.

English Translations

Förster-Nietzsche, Elisabeth, ed. *The Nietzsche-Wagner Correspondence*. Translated by Caroline V. Kerr. New York: Liveright, 1921.

Hegel, G. W. F. *On Art, Religion, Philosophy*. Edited by J. Glenn Gray. New York and Evanston: Harper and Row, 1970.

Kaufmann, Walter, ed. and trans. *The Portable Nietzsche*. New York: Viking, 1954.

Bibliography

Nietzsche, Friedrich. *The Birth of Tragedy* and *The Case of Wagner*. Translated and edited by Walter Kaufmann. New York: Vintage, 1967.

———. *The Birth of Tragedy* and *The Genealogy of Morals*. Translated by Francis Golffing. Garden City: Doubleday, 1956.

———. *On The Genealogy of Morals* and *Ecce Homo*. Translated and edited by Walter Kaufmann. New York: Vintage, 1967.

Paolucci, Anne, and Henry Paolucci, eds. *Hegel on Tragedy*. Garden City: Doubleday, 1962.

Schopenhauer, Arthur. *The World as Will and Representation*. Translated by E. F. J. Payne. Indian Hills, Colo.: Falcon's Wing Press, 1958.

Secondary Sources

Note: An international Nietzsche bibliography by this time in history could be volumes long. The brief list that follows cites only books available in English that specifically address *The Birth of Tragedy* or whose concerns relate directly to it.

Critical Studies

Anderson, W. D. *Ethos and Education in Greek Music*. Cambridge, Mass.: Harvard University Press, 1966. The definitive work on Greek music.

Calarco, N. Joseph. *Tragic Being: Apollo and Dionysus in Western Drama*. Minneapolis: University of Minnesota Press, 1969. An attempt to apply Nietzsche's categories to a wide range of dramatic works.

Dannhauser, Werner J. *Nietzsche's View of Socrates*. Ithaca: Cornell University Press, 1974. Presents the *agon* of Nietzsche and Socrates as irreconcilable, taking issue with Kaufmann's claim for Nietzsche's ambiguity and vacillation on the subject.

Danto, Arthur C. *Nietzsche as Philosopher*. New York: Columbia University Press, 1965. Contains a chapter on Nietzsche's view of art, with specific attention to *The Birth of Tragedy*. For some time a standard study, this book has been devalued by Nietzsche revivalists during the past several years.

Deleuze, Gilles. *Nietzsche and Philosophy*. Translated by Hugh Tomlinson. New York: Columbia University Press, 1983. Originally published in French in 1962, this cornerstone of the recent Nietzsche revival has an essay on the tragic for its opening chapter.

Dodds, E. R. *The Greeks and the Irrational*. Berkeley: University of California Press, 1951. Still the finest general study of the "dark side" of Greek antiquity.

Else, Gerald F. *The Origin and Early Form of Greek Tragedy*. Cambridge, Mass.: Harvard University Press, 1965. A major attempt to refute Nietzsche's hypothesis.

Guthrie, W. K. C. *The Greeks and Their Gods*. Boston: Beacon, 1950. Contains a chapter on the Dionysian religion.

Harrison, Jane. *Themis*. 2d ed. Cambridge: Cambridge University Press, 1927. The grandest edifice of the Cambridge Anthropological School.

Kaufmann, Walter. *Friedrich Nietzsche: Philosopher, Psychologist, Antichrist*. Princeton: Princeton University Press, 1974. A comprehensive study by Nietzsche's most vigorous postwar American proponent.

———. *From Shakespeare to Existentialism*. Boston: Beacon, 1959. Contains several chapters on Nietzsche's impact on subsequent writers.

———. *Tragedy and Philosophy*. Garden City: Doubleday, 1969. An attempt to trace the historical interaction between tragedy and philosophy, with several passages on Nietzsche, including a defense of Euripides, and a survey of Nietzsche's influence on later writers of tragedy such as Jean-Paul Sartre.

Lenson, David. *Achilles' Choice*. Princeton: Princeton University Press, 1975. The theories of Hegel and Nietzsche, taken in tandem, are used to derive a model of tragedy and to explain the migration of the tragic "pattern of action" from drama to other genres.

Löwith, Karl. *From Hegel to Nietzsche*. Translated by David E. Green. Garden City: Doubleday, 1964. A historical study that places Nietzsche within the context of nineteenth-century German thought.

Mylonas, George E. *Eleusis and the Eleusinian Mysteries*. Princeton: Princeton University Press, 1962. The worship of Dionysus is examined as part of a general study of Greek mystery cults.

Russell, Bertrand. *A History of Western Philosophy*. New York: Simon and Schuster, 1945. Contains one of the most vitriolic essays ever written about Nietzsche.

Schacht, Richard. *Nietzsche*. London: Routledge and Kegan Paul, 1983. Includes a chapter on Nietzsche's view of art with extensive attention to *The Birth of Tragedy*.

Silk, M. S., and J. P. Stern. *Nietzsche on Tragedy*. Cambridge: Cambridge University Press, 1981. The most exhaustive study of *The Birth of Tragedy*, a compendium of literary-historical background as well as textual analysis.

Steiner, George. *The Death of Tragedy*. New York: Knopf, 1961. Not as direct

Bibliography

a response to Nietzsche as the title suggests, this book might well be called *The Survival of Tragedy*, since it is a survey of the entire history of tragic art, ending with a once-controversial speculation about tragedy's rebirth that now seems amusingly dated.

Thomson, George. *Aeschylus and Athens*. New York: Grosset and Dunlap, 1968. A social history of Athens in the age of tragedy. It extrapolates from Frazer, Nietzsche, Engels, and Marx to achieve some very privileged insights into its subject.

Unamuno, Miguel de. *Tragic Sense of Life*. Translated by J. E. Crawford Flitch. London: Macmillan, 1921. The most noteworthy argument for detaching "the tragic" from tragedy, and establishing it as an independent worldview.

Biographical Studies

Frenzel, Ivo. *Friedrich Nietzsche: An Illustrated Biography*. Translated by Joachim Neugroschel. New York: Pegasus, 1967. A brief account of Nietzsche's life, too heavy on quotations but well illustrated.

Hayman, Ronald. *Nietzsche: A Critical Life*. New York: Oxford University Press, 1980. A well-researched and readable account of Nietzsche's working life.

Hollingdale, R. J. *Nietzsche: The Man and His Philosophy*. London: Routledge and Kegan Paul, 1965. The reigning biographical study.

INDEX

Index

Index

ABOUT THE AUTHOR

David Lenson studied Nietzsche with Walter Kaufmann and tragedy with Robert Fagles and Francis Fergusson. He is the author of *Achilles' Choice* (1975), a study of the theory and evolution of tragedy in the nineteenth and twentieth centuries. Since 1971 he has taught comparative literature at the University of Massachusetts. The author of two books of poems, *The Gambler* (1977) and *Ride the Shadow* (1979), he has also had active careers as publisher, editor, journalist, radio broadcaster, and musician, playing Dionysian saxophone with many famous blues stars.

512-2
3-15
C

672-2
5-19
C